T0181299

# Communications
# in Computer and Information Science     1730

## Editorial Board Members

Joaquim Filipe ⓘ
*Polytechnic Institute of Setúbal, Setúbal, Portugal*

Ashish Ghosh
*Indian Statistical Institute, Kolkata, India*

Raquel Oliveira Prates ⓘ
*Federal University of Minas Gerais (UFMG), Belo Horizonte, Brazil*

Lizhu Zhou
*Tsinghua University, Beijing, China*

More information about this series at https://link.springer.com/bookseries/7899

Boris Shishkov · Andon Lazarov (Eds.)

# Telecommunications and Remote Sensing

11th International Conference, ICTRS 2022
Sofia, Bulgaria, November 21–22, 2022
Proceedings

 Springer

*Editors*
Boris Shishkov
Institute of Mathematics and Informatics
Bulgarian Academy of Sciences
Sofia, Bulgaria

University of Library Studies
and Information Technologies
Sofia, Bulgaria

IICREST
Sofia, Bulgaria

Andon Lazarov
Nikola Vaptsarov Naval Academy
Varna, Bulgaria

K.N. Toosi University of Technology
Tehran, Iran

ISSN 1865-0929          ISSN 1865-0937 (electronic)
Communications in Computer and Information Science
ISBN 978-3-031-23225-1          ISBN 978-3-031-23226-8 (eBook)
https://doi.org/10.1007/978-3-031-23226-8

© The Editor(s) (if applicable) and The Author(s), under exclusive license
to Springer Nature Switzerland AG 2022
This work is subject to copyright. All rights are reserved by the Publisher, whether the whole or part of the material is concerned, specifically the rights of translation, reprinting, reuse of illustrations, recitation, broadcasting, reproduction on microfilms or in any other physical way, and transmission or information storage and retrieval, electronic adaptation, computer software, or by similar or dissimilar methodology now known or hereafter developed.
The use of general descriptive names, registered names, trademarks, service marks, etc. in this publication does not imply, even in the absence of a specific statement, that such names are exempt from the relevant protective laws and regulations and therefore free for general use.
The publisher, the authors, and the editors are safe to assume that the advice and information in this book are believed to be true and accurate at the date of publication. Neither the publisher nor the authors or the editors give a warranty, expressed or implied, with respect to the material contained herein or for any errors or omissions that may have been made. The publisher remains neutral with regard to jurisdictional claims in published maps and institutional affiliations.

This Springer imprint is published by the registered company Springer Nature Switzerland AG
The registered company address is: Gewerbestrasse 11, 6330 Cham, Switzerland

# Preface

This book contains the proceedings of ICTRS 2022 (the 11th International Conference on Telecommunications and Remote Sensing), held in Sofia, Bulgaria, during November 21–22, 2022 (https://www.ictrs.org). ICTRS is an annual event that brings together researchers and practitioners interested in telecommunications, remote sensing, and their societal implications.

We are witnessing challenging societal demands that concern energy consumption, mobility, and resilience, and we need to (i) substantially stimulate innovations related to Information and Communication Technology (ICT); (ii) be capable of developing robust information systems; and (iii) achieve reliable (wireless) telecommunications and networking. Recent years have seen a range of inspiring applications, from unmanned aerial vehicles and unmanned underwater vehicles, through sophisticated positioning technologies, to space missions. Nevertheless, there remain energy-related challenges, precision-related challenges, resilience-related challenges, and so on, which clearly justify the need for further technical improvements concerning telecommunications and remote sensing. Moreover, we lean towards the servicing perspective and the societal perspective as well, for the sake of adequately utilizing those technologies in support of people and businesses. This raises the necessity for adaptive information systems that in turn require context-aware servicing of user needs, (for example, in the case of a disruptive event such as a pandemic, much of what a person needs would change during a lockdown). Next to that, public values (such as privacy, transparency, accountability, and so on) must also be taken into account, for example, during a lockdown, personal freedoms may be restricted, which means that many technical systems should start working differently. Hence, we need a holistic view, superimposing the technical aspects of telecommunications and remote sensing over corresponding servicing-related and societal aspects. Considering these challenges brings us together in the ICTRS community, inspired by the work of Blagovest Shishkov, who established and led this conference series until his decease in 2015.

Since the first event took place in Sofia, Bulgaria, in 2012, we have enjoyed ten successful ICTRS editions. The conference has been held all over Europe, but took place virtually in 2020 and 2021 due to the COVID-19 pandemic. This year's edition brought ICTRS back to where it once started – Sofia, Bulgaria.

The high quality of the ICTRS 2022 technical program was enhanced by informal discussion on drone technology, following on from those in previous years. These, and other discussions, helped to stimulate community building and facilitated possible R&D project acquisition initiatives, which definitely contribute to maintaining the event's high quality and inspiring our steady and motivated community.

The ICTRS' 2022 Program Committee consisted of 40 members from 17 countries (Australia, Brazil, Bulgaria, Canada, France, Germany, Greece, Iran, Ireland, Italy, Japan, The Netherlands, Russia, Spain, Turkey, UK, and USA, listed alphabetically) – all of them competent and enthusiastic representatives of prestigious organizations.

In organizing ICTRS 2022, we observed high ethical standards: we guaranteed at least three reviews per submitted paper (assuming reviews of adequate quality), under the condition that the paper fulfilled the ICTRS 2022 requirements. In assigning a paper for review, it was our responsibility to provide reviewers that had the relevant expertise. Sticking to a double-blind review process, we guaranteed that a reviewer would not know who had (co-)authored the paper (we sent anonymized versions of the papers to the reviewers) and that an author would not know who had reviewed his/her paper. We required reviewers to respect the content of the paper and not disclose (parts of) its content to third parties before the conference (and also after the conference in case of rejection). We guarded against conflicts of interests, by not assigning papers to reviewers who were immediate colleagues of any of the co-authors. In our decisions to accept/reject papers, we also guarded against discrimination based on age, gender, race, or religion. With regard to the EU data protection standards, we followed the GDPR requirements.

For the 11th consecutive year, ICTRS maintained a high-scientific quality whilst providing a stimulating collaborative atmosphere.

As mentioned previously, ICTRS essentially focuses on telecommunications and remote sensing plus relevant societal implications. Within this, ICTRS 2022 addressed many research areas and topics which, as can be seen from the proceedings, fall into three main directions: propagation and image processing, adaptive solutions concerning UAV and telecommunications, and societal impacts of telecommunications and remote sensing, particularly in relation to smart cities.

ICTRS 2022 received 14 paper submissions from which seven papers were selected for publication in the proceedings. Of these papers, four full papers were selected for 30-minute oral presentations at the conference. The ICTRS 2022 authors hail from Bulgaria, Iran, the Netherlands, and Russia (listed alphabetically).

ICTRS 2022 was organized and sponsored by the Association for Radio Systems and Intelligent Telecommunications (ARSIT), being co-organized by the Interdisciplinary Institute for Collaboration and Research on Enterprise Systems and Technology (IICREST), with the cooperation of Delft University of Technology (TU Delft), Aristotle University of Thessaloniki (AUTH), and AMAKOTA Ltd. Further, the ICTRS editions are held under the auspices of the International Union of Radio Science (URSI).

Organizing this interesting and successful conference required the dedicated efforts of many people. Firstly, we must thank the authors, whose research and development achievements are recorded here. Next, the Program Committee members each deserve credit for the diligent and rigorous peer reviewing. Further, we would like to mention the excellent organization provided by the ARSIT-IICREST team (especially Canka Petrova and Aglika Bogomilova) and the support brought forward by AMAKOTA Ltd.; the ICTRS 2022 organizers did all the necessary work to deliver a stimulating and productive event, and we have to acknowledge the valuable support from our colleagues from Delft and Thessaloniki. Last but not least, we are grateful to Springer for their willingness to publish the ICTRS 2022 proceedings and we thank the editorial team for their professionalism and patience (regarding the preparation of the conference proceedings).

We wish you inspiring reading! We look forward to meeting you next year for the 12th International Conference on Telecommunications and Remote Sensing (ICTRS 2023), details of which will be made available at https://www.ictrs.org.

November 2022

Boris  Shishkov
Andon  Lazarov

# Organization

## General Co-chairs

Marijn Janssen      Delft University of Technology, The Netherlands
Boris Shishkov      Institute of Mathematics and Informatics,
     Bulgarian Academy of Sciences / ULSIT /
     IICREST, Bulgaria

## Program Co-chairs

Andon Lazarov      Nikola Vaptsarov Naval Academy, Bulgaria, and
     K.N. Toosi University of Technology, Iran
Dimitris Mitrakos      Aristotle University of Thessaloniki, Greece

## Program Committee

| | |
|---|---|
| Catherine Algani | Cnam, France |
| Mauro Assis | National Institute for Space Research and URSI, Brazil |
| Vera Behar | Institute for Information and Communication Technologies, Bulgarian Academy of Sciences, Bulgaria |
| Maurice Bellanger | Cnam, France |
| Jun Cheng | Doshisha University, Japan |
| Yoshiharu Fuse | Japan Space Systems, Japan |
| Ivan Garvanov | ULSIT, Bulgaria |
| Marijn Janssen | TU Delft, The Netherlands |
| Hristo Kabakchiev | Sofia University St. Kliment Ohridski, Bulgaria |
| Kazuya Kobayashi | Chuo University, Japan |
| Mohamed Latrach | ESEO, France |
| Frank Little | Texas A & M University, USA |
| Marco Luise | University of Pisa, Italy |
| Olga Maktseva | Southern Federal University, Russia |
| Andrea Massa | University of Trento, Italy |
| Wolfgang Mathis | Leibniz Universitaet Hannover, Germany |
| Lyudmila Mihaylova | Lancaster University, UK |
| Tomohiko Mitani | Kyoto University, Japan |
| Tadao Nagatsuma | Osaka University, Japan |
| Shoichi Narahashi | NTT Docomo, Inc., Japan |

| | |
|---|---|
| Elizabeth Nuncio | Fraunhofer Institute for High Frequency Physics and Radar Technologies, Germany |
| Mairtin O'Droma | University of Limerick, Ireland |
| Takashi Ohira | Toyohashi University of Technology, Japan |
| Yoshiharu Omura | Kyoto University, Japan |
| Jaques Palicot | CentraleSupélec, France |
| Brent Petersen | University of New Brunswick, Canada |
| Hermann Rohling | Hamburg University of Technology, Germany |
| Sana Salous | Durham University, UK |
| Hamit Serbest | Cukurova University, Turkey |
| Naoki Shinohara | Kyoto University, Japan |
| Boris Shishkov | Institute of Mathematics and Informatics, Bulgarian Academy of Sciences / ULSIT / IICREST, Bulgaria |
| Alexander Shmelev | Academician A. L. Mints Radiotechnical Institute, Russia |
| Jun-ichi Takada | Tokyo Institute of Technology, Japan |
| Hiroyuki Tsuji | National Institute of Information and Communications Technology, Japan |
| Marten van Sinderen | University of Twente, The Netherlands |
| Christos Verikoukis | Telecommunications Technological Centre of Catalonia, Spain |
| Julian Webber | ATR, Japan |
| Satoshi Yagitani | Kanazawa University, Japan |
| Tsuneki Yamasaki | Nihon University, Japan |
| Zhenyu Zhang | University of Southern Queensland, Australia |

# Contents

# Barker Phase-Code-Modulation Waveform in ISAR Imaging System

Andon Lazarov[1,2], Chavdar Minchev[3], and Ivan Garvanov[4](✉)

[1] Nikola Vaptsarov Naval Academy, Varna, Bulgaria
a.lazarov@naval-acad.bg
[2] K.N. Toosi University of Technology, Tehran, Iran
[3] Military University Shumen, Shumen, Bulgaria
[4] University of Library Studies and Information Technologies, Sofia, Bulgaria
i.garvanov@unibit.bg

**Abstract.** In the focus of the present work is the structure and application of the Barker phase-code-modulation waveform (BPCM) in Inverse Synthetic Aperture Radar (ISAR) system. The structure of the ISAR signal, reflected from a three-dimensional (3-D) object according to ISAR scenario is analytically described. Based on the ISAR signal structure the ISAR image reconstruction algorithm is derived. Based on the chip structure of the Barker sequence, the range compression is performed by a cross-correlation operation. An azimuth compression is performed by Fourier transform. A polynomial high order phase correction is applied to obtain a focused ISAR image of the observed object. To verify the analytical description of Barker phase modulation code, the correctness of the ISAR signal model and developed image reconstruction procedure, numerical experiments are carried out.

**Keywords:** Barker code · Barker phase code modulation · Barker phase code waveform · Barker ISAR signal formation · ISAR image reconstruction

## 1 Introduction

ISAR systems are effective microwave tools for imaging moving objects, on Earth, in Space and Air in all weather conditions and time of day. Classical ISARs can extract two dimensional images of the observed objects with high resolutions on both range and azimuth (cross range directions). The azimuth resolution is achieved by aperture synthesis due to the movement of the object whereas the range resolution is achieved by illuminating the moving objects by high informative wide band waveforms.

Problems of achieving high range resolution meet great interest from radar researchers for the past twenty years. Their efforts are on creating waveforms not only allowing high range resolution, i.e., having narrow autocorrelation function but to realize low level side lobes of the resolution element. There exist techniques constructing complex waveforms combine inter-pulse and intra-pulse modulations. For instance, a stepped frequency waveform is used to accomplish inter-pulse modulation, whereas phase coding

© The Author(s), under exclusive license to Springer Nature Switzerland AG 2022
B. Shishkov and A. Lazarov (Eds.): ICTRS 2022, CCIS 1730, pp. 1–22, 2022.
https://doi.org/10.1007/978-3-031-23226-8_1

(PC) is applied to accomplish intra-pulse modulation [1]. Stepped-frequency structure is applied to generate a wideband waveform consisting of narrow-band pulses to achieve a high-resolution range profile without increasing the instantaneous bandwidth. The conventional stepped-frequency waveform is Doppler sensitive. It limits its application to image moving targets. To cope with this problem in [2] is proposed a waveform with a staggered pulse repetition frequency extended to the sparse stepped-frequency waveform. A method for synthesis of interference-resistant Barker-like codes code sequences capable of finding and correcting errors according to the length of the resulting code sequence is considered in [3].

W-band inverse synthetic aperture radar imaging systems for automatic target recognition and classification due to their high spatial resolution, high penetration and small antenna size utilizing a logic-operation-based photonic digital-to-analog converter is analyzed in [4]. The V style frequency modulation (V-FM) is used to reduce signal's range and velocity ambiguity. In [5] a dual-channel, two-dimension, compressed-sensing (2D-CS) algorithm with a V-FM waveform is applied for bistatic ISAR (Bi-ISAR) imaging, solving a nonconvex optimization problem.

A framework for inverse synthetic aperture radar imaging of moving targets with V-FM waveforms is investigated in [6], where the range compression of the received signals is achieved by the dual-channel de-chirping and the azimuth compression is done via the traditional Fourier transform. Application of the multiple-input multiple-output (MIMO) configuration and the orthogonal frequency-division multiplexing (OFDM) concept to obtain high resolution for radar imagery is considered in [7].

A multiple-input-multiple-output (MIMO)-ISAR imaging method combining MIMO techniques, ISAR imaging algorithms, a special M-transmitter N-receiver linear array and a group of M orthogonal phase-code modulation signals with identical bandwidth and center frequency is suggested in [8]. Sparse stepped frequency waveforms for ISAR imaging with application of matrix completion theory is proposed in [9].

According to the theory of compressive sensing to restore an unknown sparse image from limited measurements a sparsity-constrained optimization problem needs to be solved. In inverse synthetic aperture radar (ISAR) imaging, the target's backscattering field is induced by a very limited amount of strong scattering centers, the number of which is much smaller than that of pixels in the image plane. A framework for ISAR imaging through sparse stepped-frequency waveforms is proposed in [10]. Sparse reconstruction-based thermal imaging for defect detection purposes is considered in [11]. Analysis of a bistatic ground-based Synthetic Aperture Radar System for indoor measurements is performed in [12, 13]. In case of ISAR imaging, the uniformly accelerated rotation of manoeuvring targets induces quadratic phase terms in ISAR signal. It results in time-varying Doppler frequencies and multicomponent linear frequency modulation in the cross-range signal after translational motion compensation in a particular range cell. Consequently, the ISAR image is blurring if a conventional range-Doppler algorithm is applied. To solve this problem, an imaging method based on optimized matching Fourier transform (MFT) is proposed in [14]. Implementation of wideband digital transmitting beam former based on LFM waveforms is discussed in [15]. An original SAR imaging algorithm based on no coherent electromagnetic radiation for passive SAR systems is developed in [16].

The thirteen-element Barker code possesses almost zero side lobes of the autocorrelation function, whereas its main lobe width is wide and depends on the time width of the Barker pulse. To realize a narrow main lobe and thus, a high range resolution the Barker pulse has to be with minor time width. The goal of the present work is to develop ISAR imaging technique based on a thirteen-element Barker code that guarantees not only high visibility of the resolution element but small size on the range direction.

The paper proposes a new structure for building Barker signals that achieves a high signal-to-noise ratio as a result of the lower levels of the side leaves of the autocorrelation function. All these results lead to a higher image resolution, eliminating the need for additional image focusing. In the paper, a numerical simulation experiment is conducted to confirm the mentioned properties of the wave function. The proposed algorithm can be used for visualization and detection of a wide range of aircraft including UAVs. By increasing the resolution of the images, the ability to recognize the aircraft is improved.

The rest of the paper is organized as follows. In Sect. 2, ISAR geometry and kinematics are analytically described. In Sect. 3, Barker code's structure and phase code modulation waveform is discussed. In Sect. 4, Barker ISAR signal formation algorithm is described. In Sect. 5, Barker ISAR image reconstruction algorithm is described. In Sect. 6, results of numerical simulation experiment are presented. In Sect. 7, conclusion remarks are given.

## 2 ISAR Geometry and Kinematics – Analytical Description

Consider a three-dimensional (3-D) object presented by a 3-D regular grid of scattering points in a Cartesian system $O'XYZ$. The object is moving in a coordinate system of observation $Oxyz$ on rectilinear trajectory at a constant vector velocity $V$ (Fig. 1). The geometric centre of the 3-D object, the origin of 3-D coordinate grid, and the origin of the coordinate system $O'XYZ$ coincide. The reference points are placed at each node of the 3-D grid and are used to describe the shape of the object.

The current distance vector $R_{ijk}(p) = [x_{ijk}(p), y_{ijk}(p), z_{ijk}(p)]^T$ measured from ISAR, placed in the origin of the coordinate system $Oxyz$ to the $ijk$-th point from the object space, is determined by the vector equation

$$R_{ijk}(p) = R_{0'}(p) + AR_{ijk}, \qquad (1)$$

where $R_{0'}(p) = [x_{0'}(p), y_{0'}(p), z_{0'}(p)]^T$ is the current distance vector of the object geometric centre defined by the expression $R_{0'}(p) = R_{0'}(0) + VT_pp$, where $p = \overline{0, N-1}$ is the number of the emitted pulse, $N$ is the full number of emitted pulses, $R_{0'}(0) = [x_{0'}(0), y_{0'}(0), z_{0'}(0)]^T$ is the distance vector to the geometric centre of the object space at the moment of the first emitted pulse, $p = 0$, $T_p$ is the pulse repetition period, $V = [V\cos\alpha, V\cos\beta, V\cos\delta]^T$ is the vector velocity. $R_{ijk} = [X_{ijk}, Y_{ijk}, Z_{ijk}]^T$ is the distance vector to the $ijk$-th reference point in the coordinate system $O'XYZ$; $X_{ijk} = i(\Delta X)$, $Y_{ijk} = j(\Delta Y)$ and $Z_{ijk} = k(\Delta Z)$ are the discrete coordinates of the $ijk$-th reference point in the coordinate system $O'XYZ$; $\Delta X$, $\Delta Y$ and $\Delta Z$ are the spatial dimensions of the 3-D grid cell; $\cos\alpha$, $\cos\beta$ and $\cos\delta = \sqrt{1 - \cos^2\alpha - \cos^2\beta}$ are

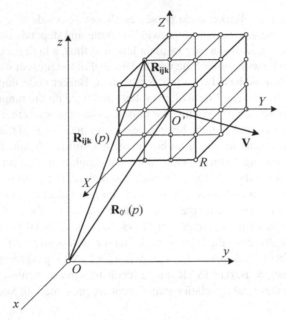

**Fig. 1.** 3-D Geometry and kinematics

the guiding cosines and $V$ is the module of the vector velocity. The indexes, $i, j, k$ are uniformly spaced in the coordinate axes, $O'X, O'Y, O'Z$.

ISAR scenario description: point $O'(0)$ with coordinates $x_{O'}(0), y_{O'}(0), z_{O'}(0)$ is the origin of the coordinate system $O'XYZ$ of the object, the position of the geometric centre at the moment $p = 0$.

The elements of the transformation matrix $A$ in Eq. (1) are determined by the Euler expressions

$$
\begin{aligned}
a_{11} &= \cos\psi\cos\varphi - \sin\psi\cos\theta\sin\varphi; \\
a_{12} &= -\cos\psi\sin\varphi - \sin\psi\cos\theta\cos\varphi; \\
a_{13} &= \sin\psi\sin\theta; \\
a_{21} &= \sin\psi\cos\varphi + \cos\psi\cos\theta\sin\varphi; \quad a_{31} = \sin\theta\sin\varphi; \\
a_{22} &= -\sin\psi\sin\varphi + \cos\psi\cos\theta\cos\varphi; \quad a_{32} = \sin\theta\cos\varphi; \\
a_{23} &= -\cos\psi\sin\theta; \quad a_{33} = \cos\theta.
\end{aligned}
\tag{2}
$$

Angles $\psi, \theta$ and $\varphi$ define the space orientation of the 3-D coordinate system, where the object is depicted, and are calculated by the expressions

$$
\psi = arctan\left(-\frac{A}{B}\right)
\tag{3}
$$

$$
\theta = arccos\frac{C}{[(A)^2 + (B)^2 + (C)^2]^{\frac{1}{2}}}
\tag{4}
$$

$$
\varphi = arccos\frac{V_x B - V_y A}{\{[(A)^2 + (B)^2][(V_x)^2 + (V_y)^2 + (V_z)^2]\}^{\frac{1}{2}}}
\tag{5}
$$

where $A$, $B$, $C$ are the components of the normal vector to a reference plane by the origin of the coordinate system $Oxyz$, point $O$, the object's geometric centre at the moment $p = 0$, point $O'(x_{0'}(0), y_{0'}(0), z_{0'}(0))$, and trajectory line's equation

$$\frac{x - x_{0'}(0)}{V_x} = \frac{y - y_{0'}(0)}{V_y} = \frac{z - z_{0'}(0)}{V_z}, \tag{6}$$

which can be described in matrix form

$$det \begin{bmatrix} x & y & z \\ x_{0'}(0) & y_{0'}(0) & x_{0'}(0) \\ V_x & V_y & V_z \end{bmatrix} = 0, \tag{7}$$

Equation (7) can be rewritten as

$$Ax + By + Cz = 0 \tag{8}$$

where

$$\begin{aligned} A &= V_z y_{0'}(0) - V_y z_{0'}(0) \\ B &= V_x z_{0'}(0) - V_z x_{0'}(0) \\ C &= V_y x_{0'}(0) - V_x y_{0'}(0) \end{aligned} \tag{9}$$

The module of the $ijk$-th scattering point's position vector, $R_{ijk}(p)$ is defined by equation:

$$|R_{ijk}(p)| = \left[ (x_{ijk}(p))^2 + (y_{ijk}(p) + (z_{ijk}(p))^2 \right]^{\frac{1}{2}} \tag{10}$$

The expression (10) can be used to calculate the time delay of the signal reflected from the object's scattering point while modelling an ISAR signal, reflected from the 3-D object space.

## 3  Barker Code's Structure and Phase Code Modulation Waveform

A Barker code is an indexed finite binary sequence defined by a one-dimensional function $b_k$, where $b \in \{0, 1\}$ is the value of the Barker pulse (chip), $k = \overline{1, K}$ is the index defining position of the value in the sequence, $K$ is the full number of values in the sequence. The distinguished characteristic of the Barker code is the small values of side lobe autocorrelation coefficients $|c_v| = \left| \sum_{k=1}^{K-v} b_j b_{k+v} \right| \leq 1$, for $1 \leq v < K$.

Barker codes are widely used in cellular communications for frame synchronization and spread spectrum. Spread spectrum Barker codes are used to construct Direct Sequence Spread Spectrum (DSSP) sequences applied in mobile communications. A Barker code with 13 elements (pulses or chips) is used for an intro-pulse bi-phase modulation of high-resolution radar waveforms before emission and pulse compression after receiving the signals reflected from the object.

Inverse Synthetic Aperture radar (ISAR) is a system for high-resolution 2-D object imaging in both range and cross range coordinates. Barker Phase code Modulation

(BPCM) is one of the waveforms used to achieve a range resolution with low side lobe levels of the correlation response while imaging. However, a high range resolution can be achieved by using short, emitted pulses that Barker sequence consist of.

Consider 13-element (chip) Barker code used for binary phase code modulation of ISAR emitted waveform with carrier angular frequency $\omega = 2\pi c/\lambda$, where $\lambda$ is the wavelength. The mathematical model of the ISAR transmitted Barker phase-code-modulation sequence in fast $k.\Delta T$ and slaw $pT_p$ time is described by the expression

$$S(k, p) = \sum_{p=0}^{N-1} \text{rect} \frac{t_{kp}}{T} exp\{-j[\omega t_{kp} + \pi b(t_{kp})]\} \tag{11}$$

where $t_{kp} = t - pT_p + k\Delta T$, $t$ is the initial time, $\omega$ is the angular frequency, $\text{rect} \frac{t_{kp}}{T} = \begin{cases} 1, & if \, 0 \leq \frac{t_{kp}}{T} < 1 \\ 0, & \text{othewise} \end{cases}$ is the rectangular function, $p = \overline{0, N-1}$ is the index of the emitted Barker sequence, $T_p$ is the Barker sequence's repetition period, $k = \overline{1, K}$ is the index of the Barker element (chip), $K = \frac{T}{\Delta T} = 13$ is the full number of Barker code's elements (chips) of the Barker sequence, $\Delta T$ is the time width of the element, $T$ is the time width of the Barker code sequence, $b(t - pT_p + k\Delta T)$ is the binary phase parameter.

For $t = pT_p$, the mathematical model of the ISAR transmitted Barker phase-code-modulation sequence along fast time, $k\Delta T$, is described by the expression

$$S(k) = \text{rect} \frac{k\Delta T}{T} exp\{-j[\omega(k\Delta T) + \pi b(k\Delta T)]\}, \tag{12}$$

where the binary phase parameter accepts values as follows

$$b(k) = \begin{cases} 0, k = \overline{1, 5} \\ 1, k = \overline{6, 7} \\ 0, k = \overline{8, 9} \\ 1, k = 10 \\ 0, k = 11 \\ 1, k = 12 \\ 0, k = 13 \end{cases} \tag{13}$$

## 4   Barker ISAR Signal Formation Algorithm

The deterministic component of the ISAR signal reflected by $ijk$-th scattering point is defined by the expression

$$S_{ijk}(p) = \sum_{p=0}^{N-1} \text{rect} \frac{\hat{t}}{T} a_{ijk} \, exp\{-j[\omega \hat{t} + \pi b \hat{t}]\} \tag{14}$$

where $\hat{t} = t - pT_p + k\Delta T - t_{ijk}(p)$, $t = pT_p + t_{ijkmin}$, $a_{ijk}$ is the signal intensity of the $ijk$-th scattering point; $t_{ijk}(p) = \frac{2R_{ijk}(p)}{c}$ is the time delay of the signal reflected by $ijk$-th scattering point. The time delays from all scattering points are arranged in ascending order. Then, summation of ISAR signals reflected by scattering points is performed in accordance with the expression (15). An index $\hat{k}$ different from this order is introduced to define the time delay $t^{\hat{k}}_{ijk}(p)$, i.e.

$$\hat{t}^{\hat{k}}_{ijk}(p) = t_{ijkmin}(p) + \left(k - \hat{k}\right)\Delta T - t^{\hat{k}}_{ijk}(p) \tag{15}$$

where $t_{ijkmin}(p) = \frac{2R_{ijk,min}(p)}{c}$ is the minimum time delay of the ISAR signal from the nearest scattering point, $R_{ijkmin}(p)$ is the distance to the nearest target's scattering point. Then the matrix $S(k, p)$ can be written as

$$S(k,p) = \sum_{i,j,k} rect\frac{\hat{t}^{\hat{k}}_{ijk}(p)}{T} a_{ijk} \ exp\left\{-j\left[\omega\left(\hat{t}^{\hat{k}}_{ijk}(p)\right) + \pi b\left(\left(k - \hat{k}\right)\Delta T\right)\right]\right\}, \tag{16}$$

where $\hat{k}$ stands for a current range number $k$ for which $rect(.) = 1$ first time for a particular $k$. It is possible for many time delays, $t_{ijk}(p)$ the index $\hat{k}$ to have the same value. The index $\hat{k}$ is considered as a space discrete range coordinate of an $ijk$-th scattering point at the moment of imaging.

Summation on $i, j, k$ indices is accomplished for each $p = \overline{0, N-1}$ (azimuth discrete coordinate) and for all $k = \overline{1, K}$ (range coordinate), taking into account the values of the rectangular function $rect[\hat{t}^{\hat{k}}_{ijk}(p)/T] = \{0, 1\}$.

The time width of the ISAR signal is greater than the length of Barker code-based emitted waveform. Denote $L = \textbf{int}\left[\frac{t_{ijkmax}(p) - t_{ijkmin}(p)}{T}\right]$ as the relative time dimension of the object, where $t_{ijkmax}(p) = \frac{2R_{ijkmax}(p)}{c}$ is the maximum time delay of the ISAR signal from the furthest scattering point from the object.

The expressions (11)–(16) can be applied for modeling Barker's phase code modulated ISAR signal return in case the object is moving on a rectilinear trajectory in 3-D coordinate system.

## 5   Barker ISAR Image Reconstruction Algorithm

First, for each $t = pT_p$ demodulation of the ISAR signal is performed by multiplication of the ISAR signal with a complex conjugated function $exp\{j[\omega(k\Delta T)]\}$. Then, the deterministic demodulated ISAR signal can be expressed as,

$$S(k,p) = \sum_{i,j,k} a_{ijk} \ exp\left\{-j\left[\omega t_{ijk}(p) + \pi b\left(\left(k - \hat{k}\right)\Delta T\right)\right]\right\} \tag{17}$$

The three-dimensional function image function $a_{ijk}$ is projected onto two-dimensional ISAR imaging plane with discrete coordinates on range $\hat{k}$ and cross-range $\hat{p}$ directions as an image function $a_{\hat{k},\hat{p}}$. Then, the two-dimensional image function can be extracted by the following inverse operation.

$$a_{\hat{k},\hat{p}} = \sum_{p=0}^{N-1} \cdot \sum_{k=0}^{K-1} \hat{S}(k,p) exp\left\{-j\left[\omega.t_{ijk}(p) + \pi b\left(\left(k - \hat{k}\right).\Delta T\right)\right]\right\} \tag{18}$$

Taylor expansion of $\omega\frac{2R_{ijk}(p)}{c}$ at the moment of imaging $t = 0$ limited by first and higher order terms can be expressed as

$$\omega\frac{2R_{ijk}(0)}{c} = \omega\frac{2R_{ijk}^{(1)}(0)}{c}(pT_p) + \ldots + \omega\frac{2R_{ijk}^{(n)}(0)}{cn!}(pT_p)^n. \tag{19}$$

A first order term $\omega\frac{2R_{ijk}^{(1)}(0)}{c}(pT_p)$ of the Taylor expansion at the moment of imaging $t = 0$ can be modified as follows. Taking into account the angular frequency of emitted waveform $\omega = 2\pi\frac{c}{\lambda}$, Doppler frequency $f_D(0) = \frac{2v_r(0)}{\lambda}$, the Doppler spectrum $\Delta F_D = \frac{1}{\hat{T}}$, where $\hat{T}$ is the aperture synthesis time interval, the sequence repetition period $T_p = \frac{\hat{T}}{N}$, the cross-range coordinate of the scattering point $\hat{p} = \frac{f_D(0)}{\Delta F_D}$, then the expression $\omega\frac{2R_{ijk}^{(1)}(0)}{c}(pT_p)$ can be rewritten as

$$\omega\frac{2R_{ijk}^{(1)}(0)}{c}(pT_p) = 2\pi\frac{p\hat{p}}{N}. \tag{20}$$

The high order term can be expressed as $\Phi(pT_p) = \omega\frac{2R_{ijk}^{(n)}(0)}{cn!}(pT_p)^n$. For iterative phase correction, the high order term is presented by a polynomial of high order. The polynomial is usually limited with a second order term, i.e.

$$\Phi(pT_p) = a_2(pT_p)^2, \tag{21}$$

where the coefficient $a_2$ is calculated iteratively using ISAR image entropy as image evaluation cost function.

Then, the 2-D image reconstruction procedure can be expressed as

$$a_{\hat{k},\hat{p}} = \sum_{p=0}^{N-1}\sum_{k=0}^{K-1}\hat{S}(k,p)exp\left\{-j\left[2\pi\frac{p\hat{p}}{N} + \pi b\left(\left(k - \hat{k}\right)\Delta T\right) + \Phi(pT_p)\right]\right\}. \tag{22}$$

The image reconstruction is a threefold operation that consist of a high order phase correction, range compression by a spatial cross correlation on a range coordinate and cross range or azimuth compression by Fourier transform.

*ISAR image reconstruction algorithm*

1.  High order phase correction

$$\tilde{S}(k,p) = \hat{S}(k,p)exp(-j\Phi) \tag{23}$$

At the beginning $\Phi(pT_p) = 0$, i.e. $a_2 = 0$.

2.  Range compression by cross correlation

$$\tilde{S}(p) = \sum_{k=1}^{K}\tilde{S}(k,p)exp\left\{-j\left[\pi b\left(\left(k - \hat{k}\right)\Delta T\right)\right]\right\} \tag{24}$$

where $exp\left\{-j\left[\pi b\left(\left(k - \hat{k}\right)\Delta T\right)\right]\right\}$ is the spatial reference function, complex conjugated to the emitted waveform.

3. Azimuth compression by Fourier transformation.

$$a_{ijk}\left(\hat{k},\hat{p}\right) = \sum_{p=1}^{N} \tilde{S}(p)exp\left\{-j\left[2\pi\frac{p\hat{p}}{N}\right]\right\} \tag{25}$$

4. Image quality evaluation by an image entropy function
a. Normalized image calculation, obtained after current phase correction

$$\hat{a}_{\ddot{k},\hat{p}} = \frac{\left|a_{\ddot{k},\hat{p}}(\varPhi)\right|^2}{\sum_{p=0}^{N-1}\sum_{k=0}^{K-1}\left|a_{\ddot{k},\hat{p}}(\varPhi)\right|^2} \tag{26}$$

b. Entropy function calculation

$$H(\varPhi) = -\sum_{p=0}^{N-1}\sum_{k=0}^{K-1}\hat{a}_{\hat{k},\hat{p}}(\varPhi)ln[\hat{a}_{\hat{k},\hat{p}}(\varPhi)] \tag{27}$$

If $H(\varPhi) = min$, end of the procedure, otherwise $a_2 \neq 0$, and go to with point 1.

## 6 Numerical Simulation Experiment

A numerical experiment was carried out to verify the properties of the developed 3-D model of ISAR signal with Barker's code phase modulation and to prove the correctness of developed digital signal image reconstruction procedures including range alignment, range compression, and azimuth compression and autofocusing. It is assumed that the target is moving rectilinearly in a 3-D Cartesian coordinate system of observation $Oxyz$ and is detected in 3-D coordinate system $O'XYZ$.

Trajectory parameters: module of the vector velocity $V = 400$ m/s; guiding angles of the vector velocity $\alpha = \frac{5}{6}\pi, \beta = -\frac{\pi}{2}, \gamma = \frac{5}{12}\pi$.

Coordinates of the mass-center at the moment of imaging $x_{00}(0) = 0$ m, $y_{00}(0) = 5.10^4$ m, $z_{00} = 3.10^3$ m.

Barker transmitted waveform's parameters: wavelength is $\lambda = 3.10^{-2}$ m, Time repetition period of sequences for aperture synthesis calculated, e.g. $T_p = 5.10^{-3}$ s.

Time duration of the Barker element in the sequence $T_s = 4.10^{-9}$ s.

Full number of elements in the Barker PCM sequence $K = 13$.

Barker element's index $k = \overline{1,13}$, time width of the transmitted Barker PCM sequence $T = 42.9.10^{-9}$ s.

Dimension of the range resolution cell is $\Delta R = 0.6$ m.

Carrier frequency $f = 10^{10}$ Hz.

Number of transmitted pulses during inverse aperture synthesis $N = 128$.

The geometry of the aircraft MIG-29 depicted in 3-D coordinate system of the object space by isotropic scattering points intensities is illustrated in Fig. 2.

The dimensions of the grid's cell: $\Delta X = \Delta Y = \Delta Z = 0.6$ m.

Numbers of the reference points of the grid on the axes $X, Y, Z$ are $I = J = 10$ and $K = 40$, respectively. Isotropic scattering points are placed at each node of the regular grid. The mathematical expectation of the normalized intensities of the scattering points placed on the target is $a_{ij} = 0.1$. The mathematical expectation of the normalized intensities of the scattering points placed out of the object is $a_{ij} = 0.001$.

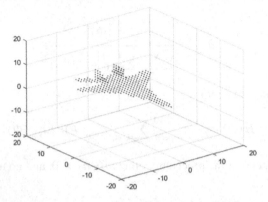

**Fig. 2.** 3-D geometry of the aircraft MiG29

ISAR scenario presented by a trajectory, initial and final position of the aircraft during the inverse aperture synthesis in three-dimensional coordinate space of observation, is presented in Fig. 3.

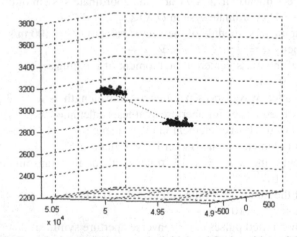

**Fig. 3.** ISAR scenario: the trajectory, the initial and final position of the aircraft

The real part of the complex ISAR signal with Barker's phase code modulation is presented in Fig. 4.

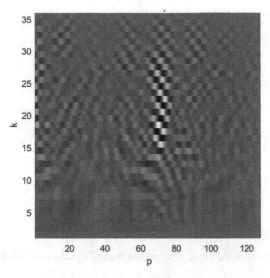

**Fig. 4.** Real components of the Barker's phase code modulated ISAR signal.

The imaginary part of the complex ISAR signal with Barker's phase code modulation is presented in Fig. 5.

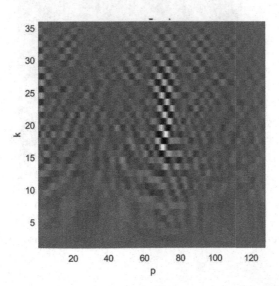

**Fig. 5.** Imaginary components of the Barker's phase code modulated ISAR signal.

The real part of the range compressed complex ISAR signal with Barker's phase code modulation is presented in Fig. 6.

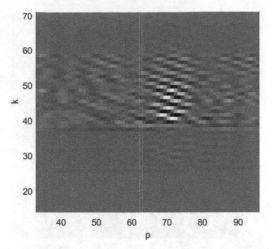

**Fig. 6.** Real components of the range compressed Barker's phase code modulated ISAR signal.

The imaginary part of the range compressed complex ISAR signal with Barker's phase code modulation is presented in Fig. 7.

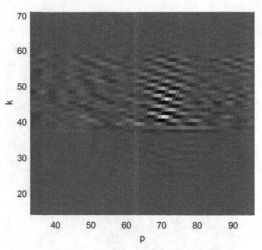

**Fig. 7.** Imaginary components of the range compressed Barker's phase code modulated ISAR signal.

The amplitude final image extracted from the ISAR signal with Barker's phase code modulation by applying azimuth compressed Fortier transform is presented in Fig. 8.

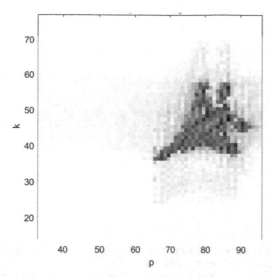

**Fig. 8.** Final image of MiG29 extracted from Barker's phase code modulated ISAR signal.

# 7 Conclusion

The structure and application of the Barker phase-code-modulation waveform (BPCM) in ISAR systems has been considered. The structure of the Barker ISAR signal, reflected from a three-dimensional object according to ISAR scenario has been analytically described. Based on the ISAR signal structure the ISAR image reconstruction algorithm has been derived. Based on the chip structure of the Barker sequence, the range compression is performed by a cross-correlation operation. An azimuth compression is performed by Fourier transform. To verify the analytical description of Barker phase modulation code, the correctness of the ISAR signal model and developed image reconstruction procedure, numerical experiments are carried out. The final image obtained by cross-correlation and Fourier transform is focused. Thus, a polynomial high order phase correction has been not applied. Software design can play an important role in the image reconstruction and can improve the efficiency, flexibility, and workability of the proposed algorithm as in [17–20]. The proposed algorithm can be successfully used for visualization and detection of unmanned aerial vehicles. The code of the Barker ISAR signal formation and image reconstruction is provided in the Appendix part of the work.

**Acknowledgement.** This work was supported by the NSP DS program, which has received funding from the Ministry of Education and Science of the Republic of Bulgaria under the grant agreement no. Д01-74/19.05.2022.

# Appendix

```
% Barker ISAR signal modeling and image reconstruction

clc, clear all, close all
load amnMIG293D.mat % load the MIG 29 aircraft geometry

% load amnF183D.mat
d = 64;
l = 5;
for h = 1:l
    amn (:,:,h) = rot90(amn(:,:,h));
end

amn_0 = amn;
alfa = pi + (pi/6) +  (pi/420);   %450, pi; % The angle
between the vector velocity and Ox axis
  beta = alfa-(pi/2);% beta = pi/2, The angle between the
vector velocity and Oy axis.

  gama = real(acos(sqrt(1  -cos(alfa).^2-cos(beta).^2)));%
The angle between the vector velocity and Oz axis, gamma
is a negative angle.

  alfaw = pi/2; %the angle between reference plane and
silhouette plane.

  alfagrad = rad2deg(alfa);
  betagrad = rad2deg(beta);
  gamagrad = rad2deg(gama);
  alfawgrad = rad2deg(alfaw);

  V=400;
  Vx=V*cos(alfa);
  Vy=V*sin(alfa);
  Vz=V.*cos(gama);
  Coordinate of reference point

% Coordinates of the reference point

x0=0;
y0=50000;
z0=3000;

%grid's resolution elements
deltax=0.6;
deltay=0.6;
deltaz=0.6;
deltaL=0.6;

%  This is 13 elements Barker's code
Code = [0 0 0 0 0 1 1 0 0 1 0 1 0]';
```

```
Nt=1;
Ns=size(code,1);
Nk=Nt*Ns;
Np=128;

F = 10^10;
lamda = 0.03;
omega=2*pi*f;

Tp=(0.5*lamda*y0)./(V*Np*deltax);

Ts = 4*10^-9; % range resolution 0.6 [m]
T=Ns*Ts;
deltaT=T/Nk;

% ISAR Geometry and kinematics
% Coordinates of the object's geometric center    at the
moment of imaging

x00 = 0;
y00 = 50000;
z00 = 3000;

[theta00,R00] = cart2pol(x00,y00,z00);
Tp=(0.5*lamda*R00)./(deltaL*Np*V);

% Coordinates of the reference point used to define a
reference plane.
x0=x00;
y0=y00;
z0=0;

% Coordinates of the normal vector to the reference plane

A0=Vz.*(y00-y0)-Vy.*(z00-z0);
B0=Vx.*(z00-z0)-Vz.*(x00-x0);
C0=Vy.*(x00-x0)-Vx.*(y00-y0);

% Coordinates of the normal vector to the plane where the
silhouette of the aircraft lies

mm=abs(V).*cot(alfaw);
Ag=(A0.*mm-B0.*Vz+C0.*Vy)./(A0.^2+B0.^2+C0.^2);
Bg=(B0.*mm+A0.*Vz-C0.*Vx)./(A0.^2+B0.^2+C0.^2);
Cg=(C0.*mm-A0.*Vy+B0.*Vx)./(A0.^2+B0.^2+C0.^2);

% Coordinate transformation (rotation) angles.
psi=atan(-Ag./Bg);
```

```
theta=acos(Cg./sqrt(Ag.^2+Bg.^2+Cg.^2));
phi=acos((Vx.*Bg-
Vy.*Ag)./(sqrt((Ag.^2+Bg.^2).*(Vx.^2+Vy.^2+Vz.^2))));
psigrad=rad2deg(psi);
thetagrad=rad2deg(theta);
phigrad=rad2deg(phi);

% Elements of the transformation matrix.
a11= cos(psi).*cos(phi)-sin(psi).*cos(theta).*sin(phi);
a12=-cos(psi).*sin(phi)-sin(psi).*cos(theta).*cos(phi);
a13= sin(psi).*sin(theta);
a21= sin(psi).*cos(phi)+cos(psi).*cos(theta).*sin(phi);
a22=-sin(psi).*sin(phi)+cos(psi).*cos(theta).*cos(phi);
a23=-cos(psi).*sin(theta);
a31= sin(theta).*sin(phi);
a32= sin(theta).*cos(phi);
a33= cos(theta);

 % Additional variables.
X=zeros(d,d,l);
Y=zeros(d,d,l);
Z=zeros(d,d,l);
x=zeros(d,d,l);
y=zeros(d,d,l);
z=zeros(d,d,l);
R=zeros(d,d,l,Np);
Tau=zeros(d,d,l);
MinNk=zeros(1,Np);

koordx=[-(d-1)/2:d/2];
koordy=[-(d-1)/2:d/2];
koordz=[0:l];
for h=1:l
    for m=1:d
        for n=1:d
                Z(m,n,h) = deltaz.*koordz(h);
                X(m,n,h) = deltax.*koordx(n);
                Y(m,n,h) = deltay.*koordy(m);
            end
        end
end

% Barker ISAR signal modeling.
tic
disp(' ')
disp('Process of trajectory evaluation is running ...')
Index = find(amn_0);
for p = 1:Np
```

```
        disp(p)
        for h = 1:1

  x(:,:,h)=x00 + Vx.*Tp.*p + a11.*X(:,:,h) + a12.*Y(:,:,h)
+ a13.*Z(:,:,h);
  y(:,:,h)=y00 + Vy.*Tp.*p + a21.*X(:,:,h) + a22.*Y(:,:,h)
+ a23.*Z(:,:,h);
  z(:,:,h)=z00 + Vz.*Tp.*p + a31.*X(:,:,h) + a32.*Y(:,:,h)
+ a33.*Z(:,:,h);

[Th,Ph,R(:,:,h,p)]=cart2sph(x(:,:,h),y(:,:,h),z(:,:,h));
                Taunew(:,:,h,p)=2.*R(:,:,h,p)./(3*10^8);
                for m = 1 : 64
                    for n = 1: 64
                        if amn(m,n,h)==0
                            Taunew(m,n,h,p) = NaN;
                        end
                    end
                end
            end

  % Minimal time delay definition (tmin)

  % minTau(p)=Taunew(49,31,1,p);
  % Bez fokusirovka
    minTau(p) = min(min(min( Taunew(:,:,:,p) )));

    maxTau    = max(max(max( Taunew(:,:,:,p) )));

    deltaTau = maxTau - minTau(p);
    Nextr(p) = ceil(deltaTau/deltaT);
    Nx = max(Nextr);

      for k=1:Nk+Nx
          tmn = minTau(p)+(k-1)*deltaT-Taunew(:,:,:,p);
  %Time dwell of ISAR signal from m,n -th point

          amnnew = zeros(d,d,l);
          phasenew = zeros(d,d,l);
          tmn(find(amn == 0)) = 0;%amn differs from zero
          S=zeros(d,d,l);
          V3=find(tmn>0 & tmn<=T);
          amnnew(V3)=amn(V3);
          S(V3)=ceil(tmn(V3)/Ts);
          amnnew(V3) = amn_0(V3);
          phasenew(V3) = omega*tmn(V3)+pi*code(S(V3));
          Skp(k,p) = sum(sum(sum(amnnew.*exp(j*phasenew)
)));
```

```
        end
  end
  disp('   ')
  disp('The process is over:')
  toc

  % Barker signal demodulation and correlation range com-
pression

  % Define the Barker code=[0 0 0 0 0 1 1 0 0 1 0 1 0]';

  for k=1:Nk
      if k>=1 & k<=5*Nt
          Sop(k)=exp(j*(omega*(k-1)*deltaT));
          elseif k>5*Nt & k<=7*Nt
          Sop(k)=exp(j*(omega*(k-1)*deltaT+pi));
          elseif k>7*Nt & k<=9*Nt
          Sop(k)=exp(j*(omega*(k-1)*deltaT));
          elseif k>9*Nt & k<=10*Nt
          Sop(k)=exp(j*(omega*(k-1)*deltaT+pi));
          elseif k>10*Nt & k<=11*Nt
          Sop(k)=exp(j*(omega*(k-1)*deltaT));
          elseif k>11*Nt & k<=12*Nt
          Sop(k)=exp(j*(omega*(k-1)*deltaT+pi));
          elseif k>12*Nt &k<=13*Nt
          Sop(k)=exp(j*(omega*(k-1)*deltaT));
      end
  end

  disp(' ')
  disp('Correlation procedure takes this time:')
  tic
  for k=1:Nk
      if code(k)==1
          Sop(k)=exp(j*(omega*(k-1)*deltaT+pi));
      else
          Sop(k)=exp(j*(omega*(k-1)*deltaT));
      end
  end

  for p=1:Np
      Skor(:,p)=xcorr(Skp(:,p),Sop);
  end
  toc

  % Imaging complex ISAR signal matrix S(k,p).
  figure
  mesh(real(Skp))
```

```
colormap gray, xlabel('p'), ylabel('k')

pcolor(real(Skp))
colormap(flipud(gray))
% axis([65-32    65+31    77-63    77])
xlabel('p'), ylabel('k')
shading flat
title('Real Skp')
axis square

figure
mesh(imag(Skp))
colormap gray, xlabel('p'), ylabel('k')

pcolor( imag(Skp) )
colormap(flipud(gray))
%axis([65-32    65+31    77-63    77])
xlabel('p'), ylabel('k')
shading flat
title('Imag Skp')
axis square

% Azimuth compression by Fast Fourier Transform

ShiftSkor=fftshift(Skor);
FFTSkor=fft(ShiftSkor.').';
ShiftFFTSkor=abs(fftshift(FFTSkor));
S=ShiftFFTSkor./max(max(ShiftFFTSkor));

save Promenlivi_Unfocused.mat...
      Skp    Sop    Skor    S    minTau

Skp_Focused = Skp;
Skor_Focused = Skor;
S_Focused = S;
S_op_Focused = Sop;
minTau_Focused = minTau;
save Promenlivi_Focused.mat ...
Skp_Focused    S_op_Focused    Skor_Focused    S_Focused
minTau_Focused

%
figure
mesh(real(Skor))
colormap(flipud(gray))
xlabel('p'), ylabel('k')

pcolor( real(Skor) )
```

```
colormap(flipud(gray))
axis([65-32    65+31   77-63   77])
xlabel('p'), ylabel('k')
shading flat
title('Real Skor')
axis square

figure
mesh(imag(Skor))
colormap(flipud(gray))
xlabel('p'), ylabel('k')

pcolor( imag(Skor) )
colormap(flipud(gray))
axis([65-32    65+31   77-63   77])
xlabel('p'), ylabel('k')
shading flat
title('Imag Skor')
axis square

% 3Isometrix image.
figure
mesh(S)
colormap(flipud(gray))
%caxis([-0.3 0.8])
xlabel('p'), ylabel('k')
%axis off

% Final 3-D image of the airceaft
figure
pcolor( S )
colormap(flipud(gray))
axis([65-32    65+31   77-63   77])
xlabel('p'), ylabel('k')
shading flat
axis square
title('Amplitude image')

The process is over:
Elapsed time is 12.859923 seconds.

Correlation procedure takes this time:
Elapsed time is 0.946830 seconds.
```

# References

1. Saleh, M., Omar, S., Grivel, E., Bazzi, O.: A modified stepped frequency phase coding radar waveform designed for the frequency domain algorithm. Digit. Signal Process. **88**, 101–115 (2019). https://doi.org/10.1016/j.dsp.2019.01.020
2. Zhang, Y., Yeh, C., Li, Z., Lu, Y., Chen, X.: Design and processing method for Doppler-tolerant stepped-frequency waveform using staggered PRF. Sensors **21**(19), 6673 (2021). https://doi.org/10.3390/s21196673
3. Riznvk, O., Tsmots, I., Noga, Y., Myaus, O.: Development of adaptive coding means, decoding of data in real time using Barker-like codes. In: Proceedings of 2021 IEEE 4th International Conference on Advanced Information and Communication Technologies (AICT), pp. 46–50 (2021). https://doi.org/10.1109/AICT52120.2021.9628911
4. Peng, S., et al.: High-resolution W-band ISAR imaging system utilizing a logic-operation-based photonic digital-to-analog converter. Opt. Express **26**(2), 1978–1987 (2018). https://doi.org/10.1364/OE.26.001978
5. Chen, J., Pan, X., Xu, L., Wang, W.: Bistatic ISAR imaging with a V-FM waveform based on a dual-channel-coupled 2D-CS algorithm. Sensors **18**(9), 3082 (2018). https://doi.org/10.3390/s18093082
6. Feng, D., Pan X., Wang, G.: High-resolution ISAR imaging with wideband V-FM waveforms. Int. J. Antennas Propag. (2017). Article ID 1908204, 10 p. https://doi.org/10.1155/2017/1908204
7. Méric, S., Baudais, J.: Waveform design for MIMO radar and SAR application. In: Topics in Radar Signal Processing. IntechOpen, London (2018). https://doi.org/10.5772/intechopen.71300
8. Zhu, Y., Su, Y., Yu, W.: An ISAR imaging method based on MIMO technique. IEEE Trans. Geosci. Remote Sensing **48**(8), 3290–3299 (2012). https://doi.org/10.1109/TGRS.2010.2045230
9. Hu, X., Tong, N., Ding, S., He, X., Zhao, X.: ISAR imaging with sparse stepped frequency waveforms via matrix completion. Remote Sens. Lett. **7**(9), 847–854 (2016). https://doi.org/10.1080/2150704X.2016.1192699
10. Zhang, L., Qiao, Z., Qiao, Z., Xing, M., Bao, Z.: High-resolution ISAR imaging with sparse stepped-frequency waveforms. IEEE Trans. Geosci. Remote Sens. **49**(11), 4630–4651 (2011). https://doi.org/10.1109/TGRS.2011.2151865
11. Roy, D., Babu, P., Tuli, S.: Sparse reconstruction-based thermal imaging for defect detection. IEEE Trans. Instrum. Meas. **68**(11), 4550–4558 (2019). https://doi.org/10.1109/TIM.2018.2889364
12. Lee, H., Moon, J.: Analysis of a bistatic ground-based synthetic aperture radar system and indoor experiments. Remote Sens. **13**(1), 63 (2021). https://doi.org/10.3390/rs13010063
13. Lee, H., Moon, J.: Indoor experiments of bistatic/multistatic GB-SAR with one-stationary and one-moving antennae. Remote Sens. **13**(18), 3733 (2021). https://doi.org/10.3390/rs13183733
14. Zuo, L., Wang, B.: ISAR imaging of non-uniform rotating targets based on optimized matching fourier transform. IEEE Access **8**, 64324–64330 (2020). https://doi.org/10.1109/ACCESS.2020.2984487
15. Fu, W., Jiang, D., Su, Y., Rong, Q., Gao, Y.: Implementation of wideband digital transmitting beam former based on LFM waveforms. IET Signal Proc. **11**(2), 205–212 (2017). https://doi.org/10.1049/iet-spr.2016.0114
16. Makhmanzarov, R., Yakubov, V.: Use of no coherent radiation for passive SAR. In: Proceedings of IX International Scientific and Practical Conference, Topical Problems of Radio Physics 2021, pp. 39–42. National Research Tomsk State University, Tomsk (2021). https://elibrary.ru/item.asp?id=47277768. Accessed 21 Aug 2022

17. Garvanova, M., Ivanov, V.: Quality assessment of defocused image recovery algorithms. In: 3rd International Conference on Sensors, Signal and Image Processing – SSIP 2020, Prague, pp. 25–30 (2020). https://doi.org/10.1145/3441233.3441242
18. Garvanova, M., Ivanov, V.: Quality assessment of image deburring algorithms. IOP Conf. Ser. Mater. Sci. Eng. **1031**(1), 1–5 (2021). https://doi.org/10.1088/1757-899X/1031/1/012051
19. Garvanova, M., Shishkov, B., Janssen, M.: Composite public values and software specifications. In: Shishkov, B. (ed.) BMSD 2018. LNBIP, vol. 319, pp. 412–420. Springer, Cham (2018). https://doi.org/10.1007/978-3-319-94214-8_32
20. Shishkov, B., Bogomilova, A., Garvanova, M.: Four enterprise modeling perspectives and impact on enterprise information systems. In: Rocha, Á., Adeli, H., Reis, L.P., Costanzo, S., Orovic, I., Moreira, F. (eds.) WorldCIST 2020. AISC, vol. 1159, pp. 660–677. Springer, Cham (2020). https://doi.org/10.1007/978-3-030-45688-7_66

# Influence of Solar Activity on the Space Environment During the March Equinox

Olga A. Maltseva$^{(\boxtimes)}$

Institute for Physics, Southern Federal University, Rostov-on-Don 344090, Russia
oamaltseva@sfedu.ru

**Abstract.** Solar activity is one of the most important factors determining the state of the nearest space, the main part of which is the ionosphere, which provides the conditions for the functioning of various technological systems. Before the start of cycle 25, there were predictions of its low solar activity and identity to cycle 24, but the behavior of the Sun indicates a departure from such a scenario. An example is March 2022. In a previous paper (Journal of Biomedical Research & Environmental Sciences, 2022), it was shown that a large short-term solar enhancement caused a global positive perturbation in the behavior of ionospheric parameters, especially the total electron content TEC, which has a large impact on positioning accuracy. This paper investigates whether such amplification is unique. The years 2022, 2011, and 2012 are chosen for this purpose. Latitude dependences of TEC for the Euro-African meridian (15° E) and longitude dependences of TEC for latitude 40° N are given. It is shown that this amplification is not unique, but a significant asymmetry of the two hemispheres is observed. The results obtained are consistent with observations by various authors in some regions of the globe.

**Keywords:** Solar activity · Total electron content · Global positioning system · Ionosphere

## 1 Introduction

The influence of solar activity on ionospheric behavior has received constant attention, despite years of research, because there are numerous aspects of this influence (and even unsolved problems). This influence is one element of space weather. Space weather determines variations in ionospheric parameters, which can be negative and positive disturbances. These disturbances have a negative effect on the operation of both ground-based and satellite systems. Negative disturbances influence propagation of HF waves depending on the critical frequency of the ionosphere, positive - on positioning, navigation and other systems depending on the total electron content TEC [1]. To mitigate this influence, it is necessary to use methods of monitoring, modeling, forecasting of ionospheric condition. Monitoring of TEC parameter is carried out by networks of GPS-receivers. The global maps of TEC obtained as a result allow studying behavior of TEC in different conditions [2], in the given case depending on solar activity. Prior to cycle 25, there were predictions of its low solar activity and identity to cycle 24 [3], but the

© The Author(s), under exclusive license to Springer Nature Switzerland AG 2022
B. Shishkov and A. Lazarov (Eds.): ICTRS 2022, CCIS 1730, pp. 23–36, 2022.
https://doi.org/10.1007/978-3-031-23226-8_2

behavior of the Sun indicates a departure from such a scenario. An example is March 2022. The authors of the paper [4] have shown that a large short-term solar enhancement, as seen in the behavior of parameter F10.7, caused a global positive disturbance of the TEC. In this paper, a study is conducted to confirm whether such positive disturbance is unique. For this purpose, March months of the following years are additionally chosen: 2011, as the year lagging on a cycle from 25 cycle, and 2012, as the month recommended by SCOSTEP [5] for studying the effect of disturbances. Similarity of behavior of solar activity of two cycles could play a great role in long-term forecasting of ionosphere parameters, especially character of disturbances. Section 2 describes the experimental data used and shows the behavior of the solar and geomagnetic indices for the selected months. Section 3 includes the results obtained. Conclusion is given in Sect. 4.

## 2  Experimental Data

This work uses solar and geomagnetic activity data taken from the website (http://omn iweb.gsfc.nasa.gov/form/dx1.html). The TEC values are calculated for the global JPL GIM map from the IONEX files available on site (ftp://cddis.gsfc.nasa.gov/pub/gps/pro ducts/ionex/) with a step of 2 h. The behavior of the F10.7 and Dst indices is given in Fig. 1 as daily mean values.

a)

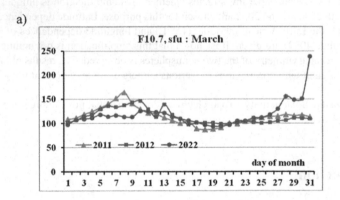

b)

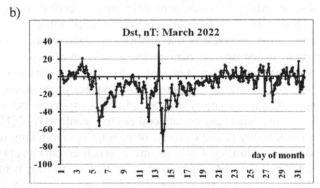

**Fig. 1.** Behavior of the F10.7 (a) and Dst indices during equinox periods (March 2022 (b), 2011 (c), 2012 (d)).

c)

d)

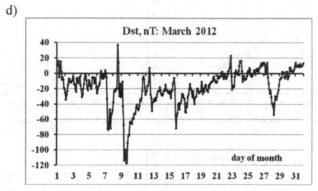

**Fig. 1.** (*continued*)

From the beginning of 2022, solar activity was fairly quiet until late March, when the F10.7 index increased first to ~ 150 sfu, and then the value jumped to ~ 240 sfu on March 31. During these last days of March, the geophysical conditions varied from fairly quiet in 2022 to a positive Dst splash in 2011 and a moderate magnetic storm (MS) in 2012 which makes it possible to estimate the effect of geomagnetic activity on the relationship of parameters with the F10.7 index. Results also will be presented for March, 28th for comparison when solar activity yet is not very big though here again in 2022 the weak MS was observed, in 2012 – a moderate storm.

## 3   Results

Figure 2 shows the latitudinal dependences of TEC for the Euro-African meridian with longitude 15° E for March 31 (the left panels) and 28 (the right panels) of each year for local time moments LT = 1, 7, 13, 19, 23. The latitude changes from 70° N to 70° S with step 5°. The experimental values of TEC (icon obs) are given together with the medians (icon med) for a visual representation of the level of perturbation.

The medians characterize quiet conditions. It can be seen that in the latitudinal dependence, the maximum values correspond to equatorial latitudes, and the minimum values correspond to high latitudes. This dependence can be explained by the value

LT 1

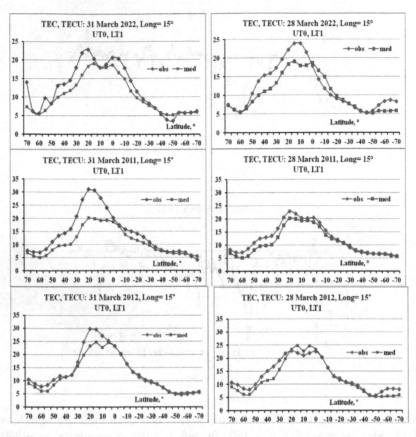

LT 7

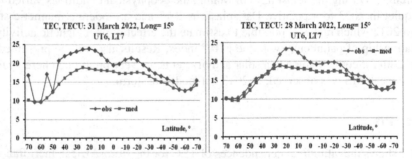

**Fig. 2.** Latitudinal dependences of TEC for March 31 and 28 of each year and several moments of local time LT (1, 7, 13, 19, 23)

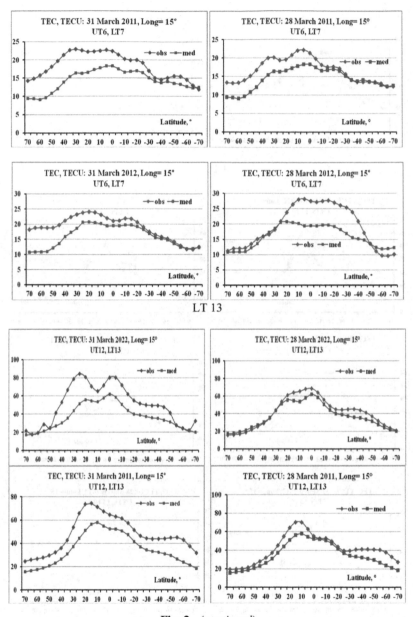

**Fig. 2.** (*continued*)

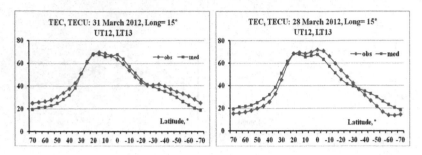

LT 19

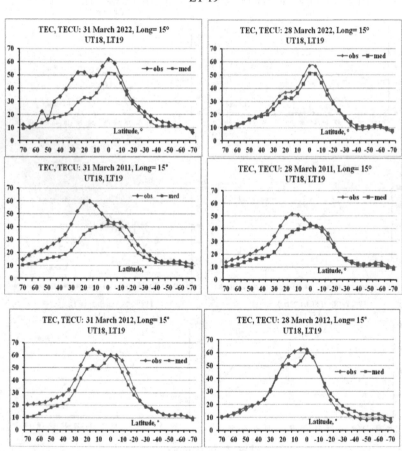

**Fig. 2.** (*continued*)

LT 23

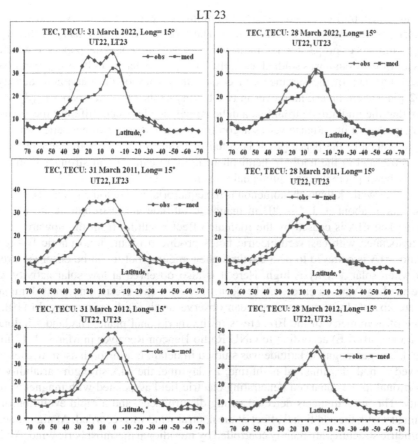

**Fig. 2.** (*continued*)

of solar illumination (insolation). It is known that solar illumination is stronger at low latitudes because of the proximity to the subsolar point and weaker at high latitudes because of the inclination of the solar rays. Consequently, the low-latitude region, where the illumination is higher, can experience a higher level of ionization. We also can see a certain asymmetry between the latitudinal dependences in the northern and southern hemispheres, associated with different seasons [6]. A significant contribution to the difference between the hemispheres is made by the non-dipole parts of the Earth's main magnetic field. In addition, the magnetic flux density is different in the hemispheres, and the displacement between the magnetic and geographic poles is greater in the southern hemisphere than in the northern hemisphere. In [7], it is shown that the magnetic field asymmetry in magnitude and direction determines the differences in the neutral wind and plasma drift in the high-latitude regions, which is confirmed by observations with appropriate instruments on satellites and calculations using the theoretical model of interaction between the magnetosphere, ionosphere, and thermosphere.

In this case, the presence of the main ionospheric trough in the northern hemisphere at night hours is the difference between hemispheres. This trough is a region of reduced electron concentration with a distinct minimum of electron density Ne and polar and equatorial walls relative to this minimum. The large gradient of density in this region strongly influences propagation of radio-waves. There are not many papers in which the behavior of the trough was studied using the TEC parameter (mainly, it is ground-based and satellite data of measurements of critical frequency or the maximum density of the F2 ionosphere layer), moreover in two hemispheres. One such paper is [8], which shows that the midlatitude trough is a delicate balance between different mechanisms, and their relative importance varies according to the existing geomagnetic conditions. With reference to the paper [9], it is noted that the troughs in both hemispheres are asymmetric and in the northern hemisphere is more evident and stronger than in the southern hemisphere during equinoctial seasons.

Another well - known phenomenon is the equatorial ionization anomaly (EIA), with two crests at about $\pm$ 15° – 20° in magnetic latitude and a trough at the magnetic equator. The EIA is caused by the fountain effect resulting from the upward vertical drift associated with eastward electric fields produced by the ionospheric E - region dynamo. EIA is believed to be a daytime phenomenon, but it can be observed even at night when solar activity is high. Here it is also observed at low solar activity, even in the median. Various cases can be seen: there are two crests, one crest dominates, both are absent. In most cases, one can observe north-south asymmetry. In [10], the change of asymmetry of the EIA crests in the meridional plane Thailand - Indonesia (longitude ~ 100° E) according to GNU Radio Beacon Receiver in March 2012 in the range $\pm$ 25° geomagnetic latitude was studied in detail. North/south asymmetries were observed at both daytime and nighttime. In daytime, the EIA strength variability was proportional to the enhanced penetrating electric field associated with magnetospheric activity. The measurements detected strong disturbances, and a rapid evolution of the asymmetry with the additional effect of the neutral wind was recorded. At nighttime, the asymmetric structures are mainly controlled by meridional thermospheric wind. Authors found direct connection between the speed of the thermospheric northward (southward) wind and reduction of the TEC value in the northern (southern) hemisphere, which is evidence of an influence from the bottom-side ionosphere.

Thus, the features obtained are consistent with the results of various authors. The main result is that the positive disturbance is observed for all selected years. This is confirmed by the longitudinal dependence of TEC in Fig. 3 for latitude 40° N. Figure 3 is given for the moments of local time LT = 14 and LT = 02, which are close to the moments of maximum and minimum values of TEC in the diurnal course. In addition to the results for March 31, graphs are given for March 28, when the F10.7 index value was well below the maximum value, for comparison. On each graph, the corresponding medians are given.

One can see that in the last days of March of different years a global positive disturbance of ionosphere appears regardless of the level of solar and geomagnetic activity. To explain this fact, we can refer to the results of the construction of neural networks, taking into account various factors. Some papers [11, 12] found the dependence of TEC on day of year (DoY) along with F10.7 and Dst. At the same time, the dependence of the TEC deviation from the median on the level of geomagnetic activity is visible, especially strong in March 2012.

In conclusion of this Section, Fig. 4 presents the results of calculations of the latitude dependence of the monthly correlation coefficients ρ(TEC-F10.7) between the TEC and the F10.7 index for meridian 15° E and the longitude dependence for latitude 40° N. The values are given for moments LT = 14 and LT = 02. Additionally shown are the maximum correlation coefficients (ρmax), which may refer to other LTs, since in some cases times of the TEC maximum may differ from LT = 14.

One can see that in the most cases the correlation coefficients are far from 1 and the night coefficients are almost always less than the day coefficients. March 2022 differs by high correlation of maximum TEC with F10.7. Low values of the correlation coefficients are connected with the influence of geomagnetic activity.

These results are close to the results of [13], in which the dependence of TEC on solar activity in the equatorial zone was studied using data from four African stations in the

31 March                            28 March

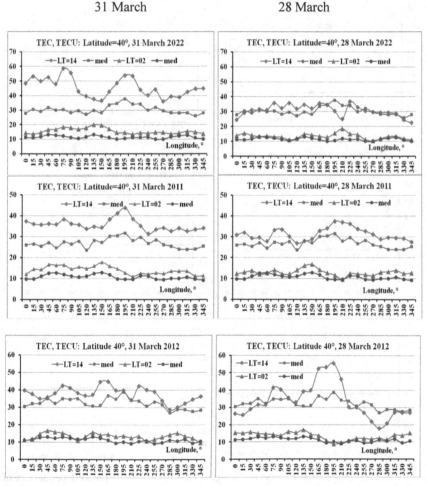

**Fig. 3.** Comparison of the longitudinal response of the ionosphere along latitude 40° N to the influence of solar and geomagnetic factors in different years.

period 2009–2016. The TEC correlation coefficients were calculated with three indices: F10.7 cm index, Sunspot Number (SSN) and EUV flux (24–36 nm), and it is important that results were obtained for different conditions: averaged for daytime hours, averaged for daytime hours for quiet days only, averaged for nighttime hours and averaged for nighttime hours for quiet days only to estimate a role of the disturbed conditions. These conditions were defined by the index Kp: ($1 > $ Kp $\leq 4$) for normal conditions and Kp $\leq 1$ for quiet conditions. The results are given in Table 1 constructed by data of [13] for index F10.7. The first line gives the station names, the second and third lines give the geographic latitudes and longitudes, and the fourth line gives the geomagnetic latitudes. The fifth line shows correlation coefficients for normal (full) daytime conditions, the sixth

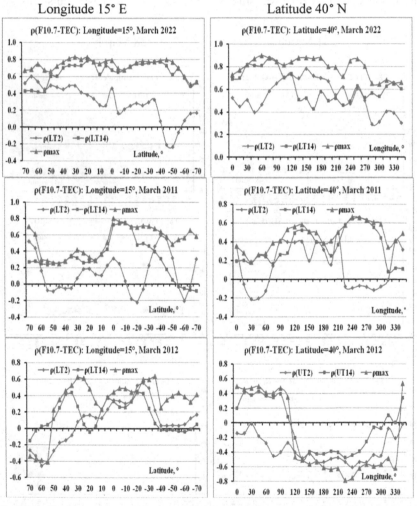

**Fig. 4.** Latitudinal (upper panel plots) and longitudinal (lower panel plots) dependences of the correlation coefficients ρ(TEC-F10.7) for March of different years.

line shows coefficients for normal (full) nighttime conditions, lines 7–8 give values for quiet conditions. The ninth line gives the average values.

**Table 1.** Comparison of TEC correlation with F10.7 in the equatorial zone [13].

| 1 | F10.7 | ADIS | MAL2 | NKLG | YKPO |
|---|---|---|---|---|---|
| 2 | Latgeogr | 9.04° N | 3.00° S | 0.35° N | 6.87° N |
| 3 | Long | 38.77° N | 40.19° E | 9.67° W | 5.24° W |
| 4 | Latgeomagn | 0.2° N | 12.4° S | 13.5° S | 2.6° S |
| 5 | Day full | 0.628 | 0.622 | 0.622 | 0.721 |
| 6 | Night full | 0.341 | 0.595 | 0.578 | 0.63 |
| 7 | Day quiet | 0.86 | 0.828 | 0.851 | 0.927 |
| 8 | Night quiet | 0.491 | 0.797 | 0.784 | 0.793 |
| 9 | mean | 0.58 | 0.71 | 0.71 | 0.77 |

Comparison of lines 5 and 6, 7 and 8, 5 and 7, and 6 and 8 shows how disturbed conditions affect the TEC correlation with F10.7: the coefficients decrease. It can also be seen that the nighttime coefficients are smaller than the daytime coefficients.

The authors concluded from their calculations that "the correlation results for the entire period consequently reveals that SSN and solar flux F10.7 cm index might not be an ideal index as a proxy for EUV flux as well as to measure the variability of TEC strength within the EIA zone". This conclusion is a matter of principle, but it seems premature to us, since the differences in the results for all three indices are minimal. A number of other arguments can also be cited. First, sunspot SSN and solar flux F10.7 are still the main ones in TEC forecasting [14]. Secondly, there is the most important problem of choosing a proxy for modeling and predicting ionospheric parameters, for which up to 12 indices are used and the EUV index is not among the top three most preferred ones [15, 16]. The results for the other indices are given in Table 2.

**Table 2.** Comparison of the TEC correlation with the SSN and EUV indices in the equatorial zone [13].

| 1 | SSN | ADIS | MAL2 | NKLG | YKPO |
|---|---|---|---|---|---|
| 2 | Day full | 0.677 | 0.657 | 0.65 | 0.804 |
| 3 | Night full | 0.352 | 0.652 | 0.626 | 0.717 |

*(continued)*

**Table 2.** (*continued*)

| 1 | SSN | ADIS | MAL2 | NKLG | YKPO |
|---|---|---|---|---|---|
| 4 | Day quiet | 0.796 | 0.781 | 0.819 | 0.877 |
| 5 | Night quiet | 0.446 | 0.761 | 0.752 | 0.771 |
| 6 | mean | 0.57 | 0.71 | 0.71 | 0.79 |
| 7 | **EUV** | ADIS | MAL2 | NKLG | YKPO |
| 8 | Day full | 0.52 | 0.528 | 0.522 | 0.872 |
| 9 | Night full | 0.374 | 0.634 | 0.602 | 0.776 |
| 10 | Day quiet | 0.893 | 0.855 | 0.853 | 0.938 |
| 11 | Night quiet | 0.504 | 0.811 | 0.789 | 0.823 |
| 12 | mean | 0.57 | 0.71 | 0.69 | 0.85 |

# 4  Conclusion

According to parameters behavior (climatological features, physical mechanisms determining the structure) the ionosphere can be divided into several spatial regions (equatorial, low-latitude, middle-latitude and high-latitude). In most publications, results are presented separately for each of the regions. In this paper, the results are presented simultaneously in the entire latitude region of not only the northern, but also the southern hemisphere. One of the results is the observation of a positive TEC perturbation both along the meridian and for all longitudes, which is not usually observed on a global scale even during stronger disturbances. At the end of March 2022, there was high solar activity: the F10.7 index increased 1.5-fold on March 28 compared to the middle of the month and almost 2.5-fold on March 31. It was shown in [4] that there was a large global positive disturbance of the TEC in both the latitudinal and longitudinal directions on March 31. The purpose of this paper was to check the uniqueness of this phenomenon which consisted in an increase in ionization due to the dependence on F10.7. For this purpose, we compared the latitudinal and longitudinal TEC dependences for the March months of three years. Figures 2–3 show that such a positive disturbance is also observed in other years, although of lower intensity. The reason may be the dependence of the relation between TEC and F10.7 on the day number, noted in the works on neural networks. In short-term, long-term forecasts, the empirical models are dominated by the linear regression dependence of the parameters on the F10 index, less often a linear dependence on the geomagnetic activity index is added, so it was natural to estimate the correlation coefficients between TEC and F10.7. The latitude and longitude dependences of the correlation coefficients $\rho$(TEC-F10.7) show the influence of geomagnetic activity, since the last days of months had different levels of geomagnetic activity, and in general all months had periods of strong disturbances. In one [17] of the few papers devoted to analysis of longitude-temporal variations of ionospheric and geomagnetic parameters at middle and high latitudes in the northern hemisphere, according the chains of various tools (magnetometers, ionosondes and GPS/GLONASS receivers) were identified "the fixed longitudinal zones where the variability of the magnetic field is consistently high or low under quiet and disturbed geomagnetic conditions. The revealed longitudinal structure of the geomagnetic field variability in quiet geomagnetic conditions is caused by the discrepancy of the geographic and magnetic poles and by the spatial anomalies of different scales in the main magnetic field of the Earth. Variations of ionospheric parameters are shown to exhibit a pronounced longitudinal inhomogeneity with changing geomagnetic conditions. This inhomogeneity is associated with the longitudinal features of background and disturbed structure of the geomagnetic field."

It testifies that regression dependences only from one parameter F10.7 is not enough to determine ionospheric conditions.

**Acknowledgments.** The author is grateful to the developers of websites: http://omniweb.gsfc. nasa.gov/form/dx1.html, ftp://cddis.gsfc.nasa.gov/pub/gps/products/ionex/. The research was financially supported by Southern Federal University, 2020 Project VnGr/2020–03-IF.

# References

1. Goodman, J.M.: Operational communication systems and relationships to the ionosphere and space weather. Adv. Space Res. **36**, 2241–2252 (2005). https://doi.org/10.1016/j.asr.2003. 05.063
2. Hernández-Pajares, M.: The IGS VTEC maps: a reliable source of ionospheric information since 1998. J. Geodesy **83**(3), 263–275 (2009). https://doi.org/10.1007/s00190-008-0266-1
3. Javaraiah, J.: Will solar cycles 25 and 26 be weaker than cycle 24? Sol. Phys. **292**(11), 1–13 (2017). https://doi.org/10.1007/s11207-017-1197-x
4. Maltseva, O., Nikitenko, T.: Impact of solar activity on the environment in March 2022. J. Biomed. Res. Environ. Sci. **3**(9) (2022). https://doi.org/10.37871/jbres1547, https://www.jel sciences.com/articles/jbres1547.pdf
5. Tsurutani, B., et al.: The interplanetary causes of geomagnetic activity during the 7–17 March 2012 interval: a CAWSES II overview. J. Space Weather Space Clim. 4(A02), 1–8 (2014). https://doi.org/10.1051/swsc/2013056
6. Perevalova, N.P., Polyakova, A.S., Zalizovski, A.V.: Diurnal variations of the total electron content under quiet helio-geomagnetic conditions. J. Atmos. Solar Terr. Phys. **72**, 997–1007 (2010). https://doi.org/10.1016/j.jastp.2010.05.014
7. Förster, M., Cnossen, I.: Upper atmosphere differences between northern and southern high latitudes: the role of magnetic field asymmetry. J. Geophys. Res. Space Phys. **118**, 5951–5966 (2013). https://doi.org/10.1002/jgra.50554
8. Castano, J.M., Natali, M.P., Meza, A.: Postmidnight mid-latitude ionospheric trough position oscillations during solar cycle 24. Adv. Space Res. **68**, 1876–1889 (2021). https://doi.org/10. 1016/j.asr.2021.04.027
9. Lee, I.T., Wang, W., Liu, J.Y., Chen, C.Y., Lin, C.H.: The ionospheric midlatitude trough observed by formosat-3/cosmic during solar minimum. J. Geophys. Res.: Space Phys. **116** (2011). https://doi.org/10.1029/2010JA015544
10. Watthanasangmechai, K., et al.: Temporal change of EIA asymmetry revealed by a beacon receiver network in Southeast Asia. Earth, Planet and Space **67**(1), 1–12 (2015). https://doi. org/10.1186/s40623-015-0252-9
11. Otugo, V., Okoh, D., Okujagu, C., Onwuneme, S., Rabiu, B., Uwamahoro, J., et al.: Estimation of ionospheric critical plasma frequencies from GNSS - TEC measurements using artificial neural networks. Space Weather **17**, 1329–1340 (2019). https://doi.org/10.1029/201 9SW002257

12. Zhukov, A.V., Yasyukevich, Y.V., Bykov, A.E.: GIMLi: global ionospheric total electron content model based on machine learning. GPS Solutions **25**(1), 1–9 (2021). https://doi.org/10.1007/s10291-020-01055-1
13. Oluwadare, T.S., Thai, C.N., Oke-Ovie Akala, A., Heise, S., Alizadeh, M., Schuh, H.: Characterization of GPS-TEC over African equatorial ionization anomaly (EIA) region during 2009–2016. Adv. Space Res. **63**, 282–301 (2019). https://doi.org/10.1016/j.asr.2018.08.044
14. Natras, R., Soja, B., Schmidt, M.: Ensemble machine learning of random forest, AdaBoost and XGBoost for vertical total electron content forecasting. Remote Sens. **14**(3547), 1–34 (2022). https://doi.org/10.3390/rs14153547
15. Vaishnav, R., Jacobi, C., Berdermann, J.: Long-term trends in the ionospheric response to solar extreme-ultraviolet variations. Ann. Geophys. **37**(6), 1141–1159 (2019). https://doi.org/10.5194/angeo-37-1141-2019
16. Gulyaeva, T., Arikan, F., Poustovalova, L., Sezen, U.: TEC Proxy Index of Solar Activity for the International Reference Ionosphere IRI and its Extension to Plasmasphere IRI-Plas Model. Int. J. Sci. Eng. Appl. Sci. (IJSEAS) **3**(5), 144–150 (2017). ISSN: 2395–3470. www.ijseas.com
17. Chernigovskaya, M.A., et al.: Longitudinal variations of geomagnetic and ionospheric parameters in the Northern Hemisphere during magnetic storms according to multi-instrument observations. Adv. Space Res. **67**(2), 762–776 (2021). https://doi.org/10.1016/j.asr.2020.10.028

# Detection of Unmanned Aerial Vehicles Based on Image Processing

Ivan Garvanov[1], Magdalena Garvanova[1(✉)], Vladimir Ivanov[2], Andon Lazarov[3], Daniela Borissova[1,2], and Todor Kostadinov[4]

[1] University of Library Studies and Information Technologies, Sofia, Bulgaria
{i.garvanov,m.garvanova}@unibit.bg
[2] Institute of Information and Communication Technologies, Bulgarian Academy of Sciences, Sofia, Bulgaria
Vladimir.ivanov@iict.bas.bg, dborissova@iit.bas.bg
[3] Nikola Vaptsarov Naval Academy, Varna, Bulgaria
a.lazarov@naval-acad.bg
[4] Prof. Assen Zlatarov University, Burgas, Bulgaria
kostadinov_todor@btu.bg

**Abstract.** The article proposes and investigates an algorithm for detection on unmanned aerial vehicles (UAV) based on image processing. The algorithm is multi-channel and detects objects at different distances from the camera. It can be used to process both standard video images and thermal images. The advantage of infrared or thermal images is that they can be applied in the bright and dark part of the day, as well as in fog or smoky environments. The results were obtained when processing a real video recording.

**Keywords:** UAV detection · Image processing · Multi-channel processing

## 1 Introduction

The rapid development of unmanned aerial vehicles (UAV) used to deliver a variety of materials and offering different types of services to improve our quality of life - cargo delivery [1], rescue missions, monitoring of hard-to-reach areas, detection of minerals, detection of poachers, search for people in need [2, 3], etc. Due to their low cost and wide distribution, they are easily accessible, easily manageable and with opportunities for easy abuse. They also prove to be very dangerous for our security and way of life, as drones currently play a leading role in military conflicts [1]. There are not isolated cases of their use for the supply of drugs, weapons, illegal materials, and objects. They can also be used to attack with explosives or poisonous materials. It is forbidden to use them around airports and sites of strategic importance to prevent unwanted accidents. Due to their small size, shape, and the materials from which they are made, their high manoeuvrability and the places of their use - especially in urban conditions, they are very difficult to detect and track.

© The Author(s), under exclusive license to Springer Nature Switzerland AG 2022
B. Shishkov and A. Lazarov (Eds.): ICTRS 2022, CCIS 1730, pp. 37–50, 2022.
https://doi.org/10.1007/978-3-031-23226-8_3

There are various technologies for detecting, tracking, and recognizing drones [4] such as: 1) Radar-Based Drone Detection. Traditional airspace surveillance radar provides stable detection of aircraft and missiles at long distances and moving at high speed, they are not suitable for detecting small objects such as UAVs that fly at relatively lower speeds and on a variable trajectory [5]. Using Doppler radar, it is possible to detect the presence of rotating drone blades, but this is very difficult, especially for a small drone. The most promising for drone detection are radar systems using FSR principles [6–8]. With these systems it is possible to detect both drones and objects realized with stealth technology. 2) RF-Based Drone Detection. RF-based UAV detection system is one of the most popular systems for combating unmanned aerial vehicles as they detect and classify UAVs through their RF signatures [5, 9–11]. The RF sensor is passive and eavesdrops on the space to detect the radio signal for communication between the UAV and its controller. However, not all drones have radio frequency transmission, and this approach is not suitable for detecting UAVs operating autonomously or with GPS targeting without RF radiation [4]. 3) Acoustic-Based Drone Detection. Relatively inexpensive acoustic detection systems use a set of acoustic sensors or microphones to detect and recognize specific acoustic models of UAV rotors. These systems are convenient to use in low visibility environments, but their operating range is less than 200–250 m. Speaker systems are very sensitive to environmental noise, especially in urban conditions or in the presence of wind. 4) Camera-Based Drone Detection.

The detection of unmanned aerial vehicles can also be done with the help of cameras. It is known that the detection and classification of UAVs is highest when the target is visible. This method also provides additional visual information such as drone type, size, and payload that other unmanned aerial vehicle detection systems cannot provide [12–14]. They are affordable, have a medium range of detection and good location of the sites. However, video surveillance is difficult at night and in conditions of limited visibility, such as clouds, smoke, fog, and dust. There are also systems using in parallel and thermal cameras to improve visibility in these conditions as well as in rain, snow, and bad weather. 5) Combined Drone Detection Systems. As we can see, each of these types of drone detection has its specific advantages and disadvantages. To improve the performance of the systems, it is possible to use a network with different types of sensors, for example: to use acoustic, optical, radar, infrared and visible cameras, etc. at the same time [2]. Therefore, maximum system performance can be achieved by merging several ways to detect unmanned aerial vehicles. However, our focus is the approach that uses camera images in video surveillance. The algorithm proposed in the article was also tested on thermal images to improve the performance of the system at night and in bad meteorological conditions.

The drone detection for the restricted areas or special zones is important and necessary. This paper focuses on the drone detection problem based on image processing for the restricted areas or special zones where used cameras for monitoring.

The proposed algorithm is multi-channel and allows UAV detection at different distances and can be used to process visual and thermal images when detecting drones both in the light and in the dark part of the day. In Sect. 2, a classification of UAVs is made to show specific characteristics of existing drones. Section 3 analyzes the proposed multi-channel drone detection algorithm based on the two-dimensional Otsu algorithm presented in Sect. 4. Section 5 shows the performance results of the multi-channel algorithm tested on visible and thermal images. In Sect. 6, conclusions and proposals for the development of the algorithm in the future are made.

## 2 Classification of Drones

For better detection of unmanned aerial vehicles, it is necessary to know their tactical and technical parameters and characteristics well. According to their parameters, drones have been classified based on their application, weight, altitude, and range, wings, and rotors [15, 16]:

### 2.1 Application

- Government: Used for mapping, agricultural needs, patrolling, firefighting, etc.
- Military: Used for surveillance, security, or combat attacks.
- Commercial: Used for applications such as aerial surveillance and photography, delivery of raw materials and artefacts.
- Personal: Used for entertainment and video recording.

### 2.2 Weight

- Nano: Drones with weight less than 250 gm
- Micro: Drones with weight greater than 250 gm and less than 2 kg
- Small: Drones with weight greater than 2 kg and less than 25 kg
- Medium: Drones with weight greater than 25 kg and less than 150 kg
- Large: Drones with weight greater than 150 kg

### 2.3 Altitude and Range

- Hand-held: Drones that can fly at altitudes of less than 600 m and have a range of less than 2 km.
- Close: Drones with an altitude of less than 1500 m and range less than 10 km.
- NATO: Drones with an altitude of less than 3000 m and range less than 50 km.
- Tactical: Drones with an altitude of less than 5500 m and range less than 160 km.
- MALE (Medium Altitude Long Endurance): Drones with an altitude of less than 9100 m and range less than 200 km.
- HALE (High Altitude Long Endurance): Drones with altitude more than 9100 m and indefinite range.
- Hypersonic: Drones with altitude around 15200 m and range greater than 200 km.

## 2.4  Based on Wings and Rotors

- Fixed Wing: Drones that resemble an aeroplane design with fixed wings.
- Single Rotor: Drones that resemble a helicopter design with one main rotor and another small one at the tail.
- Multi-rotor: Drones that have more than one rotor. The most found are tricopters, quadcopters, hexacopters and octacopters.
- Fixed-Wing Hybrid VTOL: Hybrid Drones with longer flight time. They have the stability of fixed-wing Drones as well as the ability to hover, take off and land vertically. Here, VTOL refers to vertical takeoff and landing.

## 3  Drone Detection Algorithm

From the great variety of unmanned aerial vehicles follows the numerous algorithms for their detection. In this article, a detection system using video surveillance of the airwaves will be considered. The presented algorithm in this section is original and can be used both in the visible part of the day and at night.

An algorithm for detecting drones is based on a two-dimensional Otsu algorithm, with the help of which image segmentation and subsequent automatic target recognition is carried out, described in Sect. 4. The proposed algorithm is tested on visible light images and infrared heat wave images (Fig. 1). Initially, the footage from the video is converted to a black and white image. Processing is performed both sequentially frame by frame and in parallel in several channels to detect objects of different sizes. Depending on the type of drone and the distance to it, it occupies a different number of pixels in the image. For example, a drone located at a great distance from the camera occupies a small number of pixels compared to a drone at close range [17, 18]. To detect an object in the image occupying a different number of pixels, it is proposed that the algorithm is to be multi-channel and perform parallel image processing. Each of the channels is present to detect areas of the figure with a different number of pixels. As a result of processing the output of one of the channels, it is possible to detect the presence of an object of certain dimensions. Image reconstruction can improve the efficiency and workability of the proposed algorithm [19, 20].

One of the most important parts of the algorithm is the classification of detected objects. In real-world scenarios, the detected moving objects are insects, birds, drones, airplanes, etc. In our case, indoors, we decided to use a classifier that divides all found objects into three classes: insects, drones, and background. The MobileNetV2 was chosen as the classifier. It is a convolutional neural network architecture that seeks to perform well on mobile devices.

In our next research, we will propose an algorithm for estimating the speed of the drone, based on the change in the dimensions of the drone, which are proportional to the distance travelled and the time for this movement measured by the number of frames in the video recording the movement.

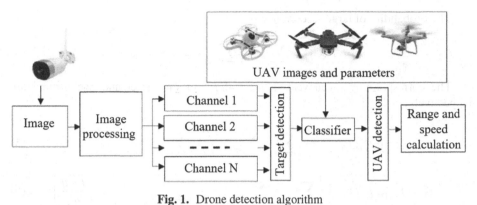

**Fig. 1.** Drone detection algorithm

## 4  2D OTSU Algorithm

The proposed UAV detection algorithm is based on a two-dimensional Otsu algorithm, with the help of which image segmentation and sub-sequent automatic target recognition is carried out. It is applied in each of the processing channels and helps to detect objects of different sizes. The two-dimensional Otsu algorithm applies the two-dimensional histogram comprising the image gray and its neighborhood image average gray to find the optimal threshold and then divides the image into the target and background [21]. Suppose an image pixel size is $M \times N$, gray scale of the image range from 1 to $L$. The neighbourhood average gray $g(m, n)$ of the coordinate definition $(m, n)$ pixel point is as follows:

$$g(m, n) = \frac{1}{k \mathrm{x} k} \sum_{i=-(k-1)/2}^{(k-1)/2} \sum_{j=-(k-1)/2}^{(k-1)/2} f(m+i, n+j) \tag{1}$$

Calculated the average neighbourhood gray of each pixel point, a gray binary group $(i, j)$ may form. If the frequency of two tuples $(i, j)$ is expressed as $C_{ij}$, then the corresponding joint probability density can be determined by the formula:

$$P_{ij} = \frac{C_{ij}}{M \mathrm{x} N}, i, j = 1, 2, \ldots, L \tag{2}$$

where $M \mathrm{x} N$ is the number of pixels and $L$ is the gray level of image, and there is $\sum_{i=1}^{L} \sum_{j=1}^{L} P_{ij} = 1$.

Assuming the existence of two classes $C_0$ and $C_1$ in two-dimensional form, the histogram represents their respective goals and background, and with two different probability density distribution function. If making use of two-dimensional histogram threshold vector $(s, t)$ to segment the image (of which $0 \leq s, t < L$), then the probability of two classes (the target and background regions) are respectively:

The probability of background occurrence is:

$$\omega_0 = P(C_0) = \sum_{i=1}^{s} \sum_{j=1}^{t} P_{ij} = \omega_0(s, t) \tag{3}$$

The probability of target occurrence is:

$$\omega_1 = P(C_1) = \sum_{i=s+1}^{L} \sum_{j=t+1}^{L} P_{ij} = \omega_1(s, t) \tag{4}$$

The corresponding mean vectors $\mu_0^*$ and $\mu_1^*$ of the target and background are respectively:

$$\mu_0^* = \left(\mu_{0i}^*, \mu_{0j}^*\right)^T = \left[\sum_{i=1}^{s} \sum_{j=1}^{t} \frac{i.P_{ij}}{\omega_0}, \sum_{i=1}^{s} \sum_{j=1}^{t} \frac{j.P_{ij}}{\omega_0}\right]^T, \tag{5}$$

$$\mu_1^* = \left(\mu_{1i}^*, \mu_{1j}^*\right)^T = \left[\sum_{i=s+1}^{L} \sum_{j=t+1}^{L} \frac{i.P_{ij}}{\omega_1}, \sum_{i=s+1}^{L} \sum_{j=t+1}^{L} \frac{j.P_{ij}}{\omega_1}\right]^T \tag{6}$$

Calculate the total mean vector $\mu_T^*$ on the two-dimensional histogram:

$$\mu_T^* = \left(\mu_{Ti}^*, \mu_{Tj}^*\right)^T = \left[\sum_{i=1}^{L} \sum_{j=1}^{L} i.P_{ij}, \sum_{i=1}^{L} \sum_{j=1}^{L} j.P_{ij}\right]^T \tag{7}$$

The definition of dispersion matrix:

$$\sigma B = \omega_0(s, t)\left[\left(\mu_{oi}^* - \mu_{Ti}^*\right)^2 + \left(\mu_{oj}^* - \mu_{Tj}^*\right)^2\right] + \omega_1(s, t)[(\mu_{1i}^* - \mu_{Ti}^*)^2 +$$
$$\left(\mu_{1j}^* - \mu_{Tj}^*\right)^2] = \omega_0(s, t)[\left(\sum_{i=1}^{s} \sum_{j=1}^{t} \frac{i, P_{ij}}{\omega_0(s, t)} - \sum_{i=s+1}^{L} \sum_{j=1}^{L} i.P_{ij}\right)^2 +$$
$$\left(\sum_{i=1}^{s} \sum_{j=1}^{t} \frac{j.P_{ij}}{\omega_0(s, t)} - \sum_{i=1}^{L} \sum_{j=1}^{L} j.P_{ij}\right)^2] + \omega_1(s, t)[(\sum_{i=s+1}^{L} \sum_{j=t+1}^{L} \frac{i.P_{ij}}{\omega_1(s, t)}$$
$$\sum_{i=1}^{L} \sum_{j=1}^{L} i.P_{ij})^2 + \left(\sum_{i=s+1}^{L} \sum_{j=t+1}^{L} \frac{j.P_{ij}}{\omega_1(s, t)} - \sum_{i=1}^{L} \sum_{j=1}^{L} j.P_{ij}\right)^2] \tag{8}$$

When the track of the above-mentioned dispersion matrix gets the maximum, the corresponding threshold of segmentation is the optimal threshold $(S^*, T^*)$, namely:

$$\left(S^*, T^*\right) = max_{1 \leq t, s < L}\{\sigma B\} \tag{9}$$

The images with noise segmented by Otsu way may get better results compared to one dimensional threshold segmentation methods, but the computation cost gets huge. That is to say, the determination of optical threshold is a function of scale value of images.

## 5  Results

The algorithm proposed in Sect. 3, basically using the two-dimensional Otsu algorithm described in Sect. 4, was tested with a video recording of a flying drone indoors. During the experiments, visual and thermal images were taken. Our proposed algorithm is used for the processing of both types of images. An XMART OPTICAL FLOW SG900 drone with dimensions 29 by 29 by 4 cm was used for the experiment (Fig. 2).

**Fig. 2.** XMART OPTICAL FLOW SG900 drone

The drone flies at relatively close distances to the camera between 2 and 10 m from it. As the drone moves away from the camera in the image, the size of the drone decreases. Due to the short distances to the drone, it was decided that the algorithm should be three-channel and to detect objects with sizes between 20,000–10,000 pixels, 10,000–2,000 pixels and 2,000–600 pixels. These areas correspond to distances of 3, 6 and 9 m from the camera. The camera we use has a resolution of $1200 \times 720$ 30 frames per second. During the experiment, the drone moved closer and further away from the camera. When processing the video, after detecting the object in a given channel, a classification of the detected object is made with images of drones known to us. In our next research we will propose an algorithm for estimating the speed of the drone, considering the time between frames in the video. Our proposed algorithm is used to process images both in the visible and the thermal range.

## 5.1  Visible Light Imaging

Intermediate results of video processing of images obtained in the visible range at these three distances (3, 6, and 9 m) are shown in Figs. 3, 4, 5, 6, 7, 8, 9, 10, 11. The figures reveal that the drone is successfully detected.

**Fig. 3.** Visual image (distance to target - 3 m)

**Fig. 4.** Segmented image (distance to target - 3 m)

**Fig. 5.** Target detection image (distance to target - 3 m)

**Fig. 6.** Visual image (distance to target - 6 m)

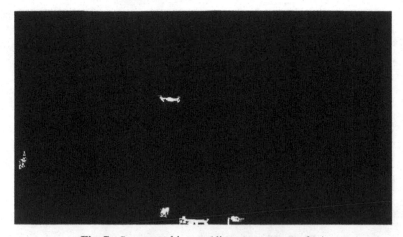

**Fig. 7.** Segmented image (distance to target - 6 m)

**Fig. 8.** Target detection image (distance to target - 6 m)

**Fig. 9.**  Visual image (distance to target - 9 m)

**Fig. 10.**  Segmented image (distance to target - 9 m)

**Fig. 11.**  Target detection image (distance to target - 9 m)

## 5.2 Thermal Imaging

During the experiment, a thermal camera was used, which registered the infrared radiation from the flying drone. Thermal imaging is suitable for UAV surveillance both during the day and at night. Using thermal images, it is possible to detect a flying UAV in total darkness and detect target through smoke. The Figs. 12, 13, 14 below show the results of drone detection with a thermal camera and the processing of the images with the algorithm proposed above at different distances (3, 6, and 9 m).

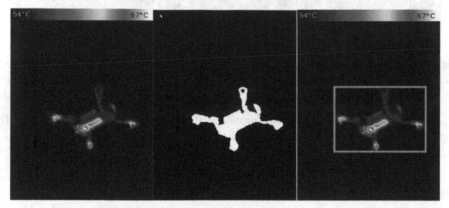

**Fig. 12.** a) Thermal image, b) Segmented image, c) Target detection image (distance to target - 3 m).

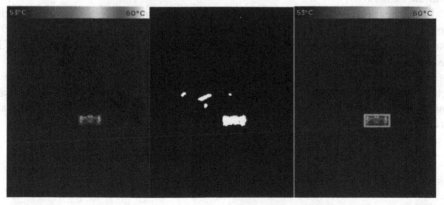

**Fig. 13.** a) Thermal image, b) Segmented image, c) Target detection image (distance to target - 6 m).

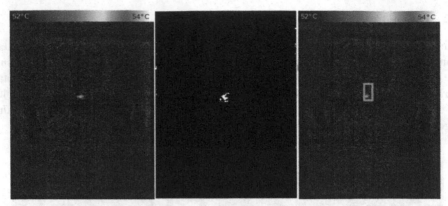

**Fig. 14.** a) Thermal image, b) Segmented image, c) Target detection image (distance to target - 9 m).

The obtained results show that the proposed algorithm in Sect. 3 can be successfully applied in the processing of visible light images and thermal images.

## 6    Conclusions

The proposed algorithm for detection on unmanned aerial vehicles based on image processing is applicable for short distances. At longer distances, it can only be used to detect objects. The algorithm is multi-channel and detects objects at different distances from the camera.

In our next research, we will propose an algorithm for estimating the speed of the drone, considering the change in the size of the drone, which is proportional to the distance travelled and determine the time of this change using the number of frames in the video.

**Acknowledgement.** This work was supported by the NSP DS program, which has received funding from the Ministry of Education and Science of the Republic of Bulgaria under the grant agreement No Д01-74/19.05.2022.

## References

1. Solanki, A., Tarar, S., Singh, S., Tayal, A. (Eds.) The internet of drones: AI applications for smart solutions, 1st edn. Apple Academic Press (2022). https://doi.org/10.1201/978100327 7491
2. Viana, J., Cercas, F., Correia, A., Dinis, R., Sebastião, P.: MIMO relaying UAVs operating in public safety scenarios. Drones 5(2), 32 (2021). https://doi.org/10.3390/drones5020032
3. Buters, T., Belton, D., Cross, A.: Multi-sensor UAV tracking of individual seedlings and seedling communities at millimetre accuracy. Drones 3(4), 81 (2019). https://doi.org/10.3390/drones3040081

4. Flórez, J., Ortega, J., Betancourt, A., García, A., Bedoya, M., Botero, J.: A review of algorithms, methods, and techniques for detecting UAVs and UAS using audio, radiofrequency, and video applications. TecnoLógicas **23**(48), 269–285 (2020). https://doi.org/10.22430/225 65337.1408
5. Güvenç, İ., Ozdemir, O., Yapici, Y., Mehrpouyan, H. Matolak, D.: Detection, localization, and tracking of unauthorized UAS and Jammers. In: IEEE/AIAA 36th Digital Avionics Systems Conference (DASC), pp. 1–10 (2017). https://doi.org/10.1109/DASC.2017.8102043
6. Garvanov, I., Kabakchiev, C., Behar, V. Daskalov, P.: Air target detection with a GPS forward-scattering radar. In: 19th International Symposium on Electrical Apparatus and Technologies (SIELA), vol. 2016, pp. 1–4 (2016). https://doi.org/10.1109/SIELA.2016.7543000
7. Kabakchiev, H., Behar, V., Garvanov, I., Kabakchieva, D., Garvanova M., Rohling, H.: Air target detection in pulsar FSR system. In: 2018 Engineering and Telecommunication (EnT-MIPT), pp. 108–112 (2018) https://doi.org/10.1109/EnT-MIPT.2018.00031
8. Che Mamat, M.A., Abdul Aziz, N.H.: Drone detection and classification using passive forward scattering radar. Int. J. Integr. Eng. **14**(3), 90–101 (2022). https://doi.org/10.30880/ijie.2022. 14.03.010
9. Bello, A., Biswal, B., Shetty, S., Kamhoua, C., Gold, K.: Radio frequency classification toolbox for drone detection. Artif. Intell. Mach. Learn. Multi-domain Oper. Appl. Int. Soc. Opt. Photonics **11006**, 110061Y (2019). https://doi.org/10.1117/12.2514759
10. Raja Abdullah, R.S.A., Abdul Aziz, N.H., Abdul Rashid, N.E., Ahmad Salah, A., Hashim, F.: Analysis on target detection and classification in LTE based passive forward scattering radar. Sensors **2016**(16), 1607 (2016). https://doi.org/10.3390/s16101607
11. Raja Abdullah, R.S.A., Alhaji Musa, S., Abdul Rashid, N.E., Sali, A., Salah, A.A., Ismail, A.: Passive forward-scattering radar using digital video broadcasting satellite signal for drone detection. Remote Sens. **2020**(12), 3075 (2020). https://doi.org/10.3390/rs12183075
12. Marin, F-B., Marin M.: Drone detection using image processing based on deep learning. The Annals of "Dunarea de Jos" University of Galati. Fascicle IX, Metallurgy and Materials Science, no. 4 (2021). https://doi.org/10.35219/mms.2021.4.06
13. Samadzadegan, F., Javan, F., Mahini, F., Gholamshahi, M.: Detection and recognition of drones based on a deep convolutional neural network using visible imagery. Aerospace **9**(1), 31 (2022). https://doi.org/10.3390/aerospace9010031
14. Seidaliyeva, U., Akhmetov, D., Ilipbayeva, L., Matson, E.T.: Real-time and accurate drone detection in a video with a static background. Sensors **2020**(20), 3856 (2022). https://doi.org/ 10.3390/s20143856
15. Chamola, V., Kotesh, P., Agarwal, A., Naren, G. N., Guizani, M.: A comprehensive review of unmanned aerial vehicle attacks and neutralization techniques. Ad Hoc Netw. **111**, 102324 (2021). https://doi.org/10.1016/j.adhoc.2020.102324
16. PS, R., Jeyan, M.L.: Mini Unmanned Aerial Systems (UAV) - a review of the parameters for classification of a mini UAV. Int. J. Aviat. Aeronaut. Aerosp. **7**(3) (2020). https://doi.org/10. 15394/ijaaa.2020.1503
17. Pham, G., Nguyen, P.: Drone detection experiment based on image processing and machine learning. Int. J. Sci. Technol. Res. **9**(2) (2020). ISSN 2277-8616
18. Li, B., Qiu, S., Jiang, W., Zhang, W., Le, M.: A UAV detection and tracking algorithm based on image feature super-resolution. Wireless Commun. Mob. Comput. **2022**, 8 pages (2022). Article ID 6526684. https://doi.org/10.1155/2022/6526684
19. Garvanova, M., Ivanov, V.: Quality assessment of defocused image recovery algorithms. In: 3rd International Conference on Sensors, Signal and Image Processing – SSIP 2020, 23–25 October 2020, Prague, Czech Republic, pp. 25–30. New York, NY, USA: Association for Computing Machinery (2020). ISBN 978-1-4503-8828-3. https://doi.org/10.1145/3441233. 3441242

20. Garvanova, M., Ivanov, V.: Quality assessment of image deburring algorithms. In: IOP Conference Series: Materials Science and Engineering, vol. 1031, no. 1, pp. 1–5 (2021). Print ISSN 1757-8981, Online ISSN 1757–899X. https://doi.org/10.1088/1757-899X/1031/1/012051

21. Kumar, K., Kavitha, G., Subramanian, R., Ramesh, G.: Visual and thermal image fusion for UAV based target tracking, in MATLAB - A Ubiquitous Tool for the Practical Engineer. London, United Kingdom: IntechOpen (2011). https://doi.org/10.5772/23996

# Combining Context-Awareness and Data Analytics in Support of Drone Technology

Boris Shishkov[1,2,3]([⊠]), Krassimira Ivanova[1], Alexander Verbraeck[4], and Marten van Sinderen[5]

[1] Institute of Mathematics and Informatics, Bulgarian Academy of Sciences, Sofia, Bulgaria
kivanova@math.bas.bg
[2] Faculty of Information Sciences, University of Library Studies and Information Technologies, Sofia, Bulgaria
[3] Institute IICREST, Sofia, Bulgaria
b.b.shishkov@iicrest.org
[4] Faculty of Technology, Policy, and Management, Delft University of Technology, Delft, The Netherlands
a.verbraeck@tudelft.nl
[5] Faculty of Electrical Engineering, Mathematics and Computer Science, University of Twente, Enschede, The Netherlands
m.j.vansinderen@utwente.nl

**Abstract.** Drones performing an autonomous mission need to adapt to frequent changes in their environment. In other words, they have to be context-aware. Most current context-aware systems are designed to distinguish between situations that have been pre-defined in terms of anticipated situation types and corresponding desired behavior types. This only partially benefits drone technology because many types of drone missions can be characterized by situations that are hard to predict at design time. We suggest combining context-awareness and data analytics for a better situation coverage. This could be achieved by using performance data (generated at real-time) as training data for supervised machine learning – it would allow relating situations to appropriate behaviors that a drone could follow. The conceptual ideas are presented in this position paper while validation is left for future work.

**Keywords:** Drone technology · Context-awareness · Data analytics

## 1 Introduction

We address Unmanned Aerial Vehicles (UAV) [1] with the label "drones" in the remainder of this paper. As studied in [2–12]: (i) Drones are capable of replacing people in dangerous environments and can make use of advanced sensing capabilities allowing for situational awareness. (ii) Drones are available in different sizes – small ones can reach difficult to access places; larger drones can monitor buildings, cities, or regions for many hours in a row. (iii) Drones need to be able to adapt to changes in their environment, while performing their missions. This makes context-awareness [13, 14] relevant

© The Author(s), under exclusive license to Springer Nature Switzerland AG 2022
B. Shishkov and A. Lazarov (Eds.): ICTRS 2022, CCIS 1730, pp. 51–60, 2022.
https://doi.org/10.1007/978-3-031-23226-8_4

to drone technology. Context awareness essentially concerns adaptive service delivery [15], for which three adaptation perspectives are possible: serving user needs, system needs, and public values [16]. Most current context-aware systems are specified to distinguish between several anticipated situation types that have been defined at design time, this leading to triggering corresponding desired behavior types [17, 18].

Nevertheless, this only partially benefits drone technology because drone missions are often carried out in difficult situations [12] and therefore they can suffer from situations that are hard to predict at design time. We suggest combining context-awareness and data analytics [19] for a better situation coverage. This could be achieved by using performance data (generated at real-time) as training data for supervised machine learning, which would allow the drone to apply appropriate behaviors in similar situations.

We refer to literature and previous work (see above) for the topics of drone technology and context-awareness, presenting our ideas on top of that. Validation is left for future work.

The remaining of the paper is structured as follows: Sect. 2 covers drone technology from a functional perspective. Section 3 presents a context-awareness conceptual model. In Sect. 4 we present our proposed conceptual framework. Finally, in Sect. 5, we discuss the framework and its limitations as well as our plans for future work.

## 2  Drone Technology – A Functional Perspective

Extensive literature exists about architectures for autonomous systems, with a nice overview in [2–12]. In this position paper, we mainly focus on the design choices for a drone system that relate to societal demands [20–22] and governance [23], as well as the technical capabilities of the drone [5]. In this, we view a drone as AGENT, in the

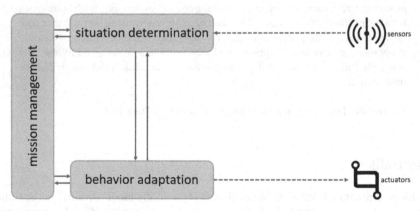

**Fig. 1.** Drone technology – a functional perspective

category of Multi-Agent Systems, referring to Wooldridge [24]. As such, the drone is *autonomous to some degree and adaptive, and has **three key features***, namely: (i) The ability to gather relevant contextual information by means of *sensing*; (ii) The ability to analyze this data (and possibly generate conclusions and/or decisions), by means of *algorithms*; (iii) The ability to adapt its behavior in *response to changes in the environment*. This is visualized (inspired by previous work [2]) in Fig. 1.

As Fig. 1 suggests, drones are essentially driven by a corresponding mission and mission management is hence crucial. It is sensitive to the "current" situation that is to be somehow determined by the drone – this is often done by means of reasoning on data from sensors. The mission management also concerns the drone's behavior adaptation. In summary, it is necessary for a drone to get relevant information (for the sake of determining the "current" situation) and be able to adapt its behavior accordingly (for the sake of delivering situation-specific services); as it concerns the former/latter, a drone would count on sensors/actuators.

## 3 Context-Awareness

As a problem theory for *context-aware* systems we postulate that *end-users* (*users*, for short) of *information systems* often have different needs for services provided by such systems, where different needs correspond to different context situations. As studied in [13], *context-aware* (information) systems are a "treatment" for this problem if they can provide **context-specific services to users in accordance to their context-dependent needs** [25–39]. "Context" here is the *context* of the *context-aware* system, where the former is a given (i.e., not designed) and the latter is the object of design. A *context-aware* system that is transferred to practice would interact with its context. Two kinds of interactions can be distinguished: one for *collecting data on the context* and another one - for *delivering a service* that matches the *context*. The fact that the *service* is delivered to a *user* means that the user is part of the context. This makes perfect sense, as the *part-of* relation is an essential prerequisite for the system we want to design, viz. to make a connection between what the *context* is and what a *user* needs.

We frame the design problem with the diagram in Fig. 2. The diagram shows that a **user**, being *part of* a **context**, has *one or more* **user need**s (or sets of *user needs*), where each distinguished *user need* results from a corresponding unique **context situation**. A *context* can be conceived as a *temporal composition of one or more context situations*, where each *context situation* has a unique set of *properties* that collectively are relevant to a specific *user need*. A useful **context-aware system** is able to detect the *context situation* at hand and then offers one or more **situation-specific services** that satisfy the *needs* of the *user* being in, or experiencing, that situation.

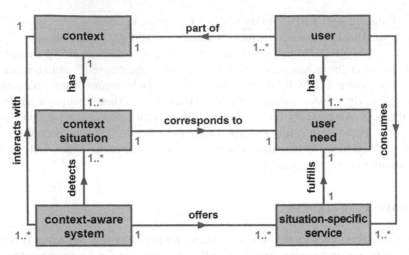

**Fig. 2.** Framing the problem of context-awareness (Source: [13], p. 122 ©2021, Springer, reprinted with permission)

## 4  Solution Directions

In the current paper, we consider **_drones_** viewed as a **_context-aware system_** (in general) and in particular – their role for the benefit of mitigations after disruptive events, such as natural disasters, pandemics, military conflicts, and so on [2], sticking to **_Systemics_** [14, 15, 21]. As visualized in Fig. 3, where the grey area stays for our system of consideration, we emphasize on _system-user interaction_ (indicated at the bottom of the figure) and on the _environmental input signals_, (indicated at the top of the figure); for the sake of brevity, we omit the unavoidable reflection of system behavior to the environment. Further, taking a functional holistic perspective on a drone system, we abstract from the system duality vision assuming two overlapping systems, namely the one responsible for _motion planning_ and the other one – for the achievement of concrete _goals_.

We suggest envisioning **two systems** (**SA** and **SB**) that complement each other, as inter-related parts of the drone system of consideration, as visualized in Fig. 3 (arrows indicate corresponding data flows; "**_CA_**" stands for "_context-awareness_" and "**_DA_**" stands for "_data analytics_"):

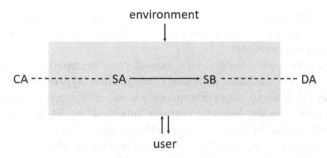

**Fig. 3.** A vision for combining context-awareness and data analytics

*SA has been designed to distinguish between different situations* that concern the user/environment, in the sense that SA is *capable of capturing a number of data values* (for example: sensor readings) whose combination points to the "current" situation type. Then SA would *trigger accordingly a corresponding behavior type*. We may take another perspective on this: (i) There are a number of possible SITUATION INSTANCES that are recognizable by the systems and those instances are characterized by corresponding ATTRIBUTE VALUES; (ii) The different possible system behaviors are in (several) behavior CLASSES and *AS PRE-DEFINED AT DESIGN TIME*: *for each recognizable situation instance there is a corresponding desirable behavior class*. For example, there may be three behavior classes relevant to the drone-mitigation case, namely: MONITOR, BRING THINGS, and FLY BACK. As it concerns situations, there may be relevant attributes, such as (suffering) person(s) identified: Yes or No; the drone has enough power (fuel and/or battery): Yes or No; there is overall emergency: Yes or No; drone supplies are: normal, scares, or none, and so on; the identified person(s) are: in close proximity to the drone, in mid proximity, or away, and so on. Hence, depending on the values, we derive an INSTANCE TUPLE and for each *instance tuple*, SA "knows" which *behavior class* to trigger. This all is rooted in the *CA paradigm* (see the dashed line at the left side of Fig. 3 and refer to Sect. 3) and validated in many cases, such as AWARENESS [40].

We argue that using this alone would mean that we should: (i) either *spend too much time and resources during the design*, for identifying, specifying, and designing things that concern very many potential *situation instances*; (ii) or *assume high levels of risk that a situation instance would pop up that cannot be "recognized" by the system*. Systems servicing critical enterprises would count on developments that are backed by "huge" resources and (i) would then be realistic, which we nevertheless consider not the case as it concerns most current civil drone systems.

Hence, we count on *SB*, rooted in *DA* (see the dashed line at the right side of the Figure), to complement *SA* in a useful way, considering *SML - Supervised Machine Learning* [19] and *Statistics* [41]. In particular, the "running" of *SA* would produce "for free" as "side effect" *training data that would feed SB*. Since this would be *labelled data*, it would adequately let *SB learn to dynamically compose behaviors* for situations not recognized by *SA*. Still, this all should "happen" at a *lower granularity level*, assuming that *situation instances* point to particular *attribute values* that are considered by *SB*.

When *SA* has not "recognized" a situation instance, it could at least pass to *SB attribute-values-level data* concerning what was captured. This can be used by *SB* to "decide" **which behavior class to trigger**.

In referring to *SML* and *Statistics*, let us consider (for example) *CovA* – the *Covering Algorithm* and *BCA* – the *Naïve Bayesian Classification Approach* [43]. In applying *CovA*, *SB* uses the *training data* (in terms of a number of *tuples*, featuring *situation instances* and corresponding *behavior classes*) "inherited" by *SA*, to generate **RULES** corresponding to each of the *behavior classes*. Hence, in the event of *SA* not recognizing a *situation instance*, it "goes" to *SB* which in turn applies the abovementioned *rules* to it in order to establish a match with regard to one of the *behavior classes*, triggering it accordingly. In applying *BCA*, *SB* similarly uses the *training data* (see above) but in a different way and restricted by the *BCA* limitation of considering maximum two *behavior classes*. Then it would be a question which of the two *behavior classes* is more adequate with regard to the *situation instance* that has not been recognized by *SA*. To answer this question for the benefit of *SB*, we need to apply the *Bayes Theorem* that allows for classifying a *tuple* (featuring a *situation instance*) with regard to two *behavior classes*, using the abovementioned *training data*. That is how *SB* would identify the relevant *behavior class* and would trigger it accordingly. And in the end, even though *Neural Networks* [42] can bring invaluable pattern-recognition-related support to drone's motion planning, we argue that methods, such as the ones considered above (and possibly also *decision-tree classifiers* [19]) are most appropriate for combining *CA* and *DA*. That is not only because the *attributes* are precisely defined by *SA* but also because traceability is important - the system "decisions" have to be explainable.

Further, it would be possible "exporting" *SA*'s *training data* to other systems and/or "importing" (for the benefit of *SB*) external *training data*. Nevertheless, for this the *training data* STRUCTURE (featured by particular *attributes*) should be the same – for example, if *SA* is recognizing situations, considering particular *attributes* while later *SB* would be covering unrecognized situations, considering other *attributes*, then the overall *quality-of-service* would be low and with limited *traceability* potential. Also, we must not forget the existence of the problem of confusion between *causality* and *coincidence*. Finally, *SB*'s *inheriting* classification models from other *CA* (*drone*) *systems* poses the need for addressing, issues, such as *data reliability*, *data pre-processing*, *data harmonization*, and so on.

In summary, going back to the example featuring *drones used for monitoring that aims at mitigations after disruptive events* [2], we have just two *behavior classes*, namely: *monitoring of people in normal health in an affected area* (when just monitoring is needed), and *providing support to persons needing urgent help in this area*. Here, at a lower granularity level we may consider values of attributes featuring the *health situation*, the *area*, and so on. Hence, a *situation instance* unrecognized by *SA* and hence "passed" to *SB* would be: *a person needs urgent help outside of the affected area* (for instance – when the drone can identify some accident outside of the area which is on the focus of its mission). Then, with this not having been anticipated at design time, *SB* may try to identify the right *behavior class* to trigger, for example, by applying *CovA* or *BCA* (see above), possibly resulting in: *call ambulance*.

Hence, there are several things that are essential: • the (drone) system (and in particular *SA*) should be capable of identifying situation instances; • in this, its possibilities are not unlimited, in the sense that only a limited number of situation instances (these anticipated at design time) are covered; • for each recognized situation instance, the system (and in particular *SA*) switches to a corresponding behavior class (and this was also "prepared" at design time); • any unrecognized situation instance is to be "passed" to *SB*; • it uses training data (in terms of tuples featuring situation instances and reflecting corresponding attribute values and a relevant behavior class) "inherited" by *SA*; • in this, *SB* applies *CovA*, *BCA*, or another appropriate method for classifying the situation instance with regard to the behavior classes.

## 5 Discussion and Conclusions

Nowadays, drones have become indispensable helpers in many situations, from various observations to detect damage in critical infrastructures such as roads, railways, or other facilities, through monitoring featuring flooded areas, agricultural crops, pollution spots, and deforestation, to active actions such as delivering first aid kits and spraying insecticides.

A specific feature of such missions (that are often carried out in difficult situations) is the *dynamic change in environment*, and it is often *impossible to foresee all scenarios at design time*. This is specific even though not exclusively valid for drones and concerns such context-awareness-related limitations. Still, the contribution of the current paper is limited to *drone technology*.

We have addressed this technology, referring to previous work and we have superimposed this with regard to a *context-awareness* conceptualization (again referring to previous work). On that basis, we have proposed solution directions featuring the *combined application of context-aware computing and data analytics*, and assuming a *system duality*, as follows:

- The first one is a "classical" context-aware system, which *incorporates recognition of different situations and sets appropriate behaviors* according to algorithms established at design time.
- Unlike the classical system, whose functions end there, in the proposed architecture, *this system feeds data, characterizing situations and behaviors to a second system*; those recognizable cases will be used by the second system to *build a classification model, such that it is capable of generating rules in a cases when the first system falls into a "non-recognized" situation*.

*Validating* the proposed idea is left for future work.
The *limitations* of our work are considered to be three-fold:

- An explicit discussion is missing concerning the *criteria for "calling SB"* since it may be that a situation is not "recognized" because of sensor failures and/or data-processing-related issues.

- A *mapping architecture* is missing as it concerns the two granularity levels, namely: the *SA* granularity level featuring *situations* and *behaviors*, and the *SB* granularity level featuring *patterns* of both.
- The work is limited just to *drone technology*.

**Acknowledgement.** This work was partially supported by: (i) Contract "NGIC – National Geoinformation Center for monitoring, assessment and prediction natural and anthropogenic risks and disasters" under the Program "National Roadmap for Scientific Infrastructure 2017–2023", financed by Bulgarian Ministry of Education and Science; (ii) Faculty of Technology, Policy, and Management – Delft University of Technology; (iii) Faculty of Electrical Engineering, Mathematics and Computer Science – University of Twente.

# References

1. Griffin, G.F.: The use of unmanned aerial vehicles for disaster management. Geomatica **68**(4), 265–281 (2014)
2. Shishkov, B., Branzov, T., Ivanova, K., Verbraeck, A.: Using drones for resilience: a system of systems perspective. In: Proceedings of the 10th International Conference on Telecommunications and Remote Sensing (ICTRS 2021), New York, NY, USA. Association for Computing Machinery (2021)
3. Shishkov, B., Hristozov, S., Verbraeck, A.: Improving resilience using drones for effective monitoring after disruptive events. In: Proceedings of the 9th International Conference on Telecommunications and Remote Sensing (ICTRS 2020), New York, NY, USA. Association for Computing Machinery (2020)
4. Shishkov, B., Hristozov, S., Janssen, M., Van Den Hoven, J.: Drones in land border missions: benefits and accountability concerns. In: Proceedings of the 6th International Conference on Telecommunications and Remote Sensing (ICTRS 2017), New York, NY, USA. Association for Computing Machinery (2017)
5. Milas, A.S., Cracknell, A.P., Warner, T.A.: Drones – the third generation source of remote sensing data. Int. J. Remote Sens. **39**(21), 7125–7137 (2018)
6. Kayan, H., Eslampanah, R., Yeganli, F., Askar, M.: Heat leakage detection and surveillance using aerial thermography drone. In: Proceedings of the 26th Signal Processing and Communications Applications Conference (SIU) (2018)
7. Pandey, S., Barik, R.K., Gupta, S., Arthi, R.: Pandemic drone with thermal imaging and crowd monitoring system (DRISHYA). In: Tripathy, H.K., Mishra, S., Mallick, P.K., Panda, A.R. (eds.) Technical Advancements of Machine Learning in Healthcare. SCI, vol. 936, pp. 307–325. Springer, Singapore (2021). https://doi.org/10.1007/978-981-33-4698-7_15
8. Hill, A.C., Laugier, E.J., Casana, J.: Archaeological remote sensing using multi-temporal, drone-acquired thermal and Near Infrared (NIR) imagery: a case study at the Enfield Shaker Village, New Hampshire. Remote Sens. **12**(4), 690 (2020)
9. Carrio, A., Sampedro, C., Rodriguez-Ramos, A., Campoy, P.: A review of deep learning methods and applications for unmanned aerial vehicles. J. Sens. **2017**, Article ID 3296874 (2017)
10. Erdelj, M., Natalizio, E., Chowdhury, K.R., Akyildiz, I.F.: Help from the sky: leveraging UAVs for disaster management. IEEE Pervasive Comput. **16**(1), 24–32 (2017)

11. Kopardekar, P., Rios, J., Prevot, Th., Johnson, M., Jung, J., Robinson III, J.E.: Unmanned aircraft system traffic management (UTM) concept of operations. In: Proceedings of the 16th AIAA Aviation Technology, Integration, and Operations Conference, Washington, D.C., USA (2016)

12. American Red Cross: Drones for Disaster Response and Relief Operations (2015). https://www.issuelab.org/resources/21683/21683.pdf

13. Shishkov, B., van Sinderen, M.: Towards well-founded and richer context-awareness conceptual models. In: Shishkov, B. (ed.) BMSD 2021. LNBIP, vol. 422, pp. 118–132. Springer, Cham (2021). https://doi.org/10.1007/978-3-030-79976-2_7

14. Shishkov, B., van Sinderen, M.: On the context-aware servicing of user needs: extracting and managing context information supported by rules and predictions. In: Shishkov, B. (eds.) BMSD 2022. LNBIP, vol. 453, pp. 240–248. Springer, Cham (2022) https://doi.org/10.1007/978-3-031-11510-3_15

15. Shishkov, B.: Designing Enterprise Information Systems, Merging Enterprise Modeling and Software Specification. Springer, Cham (2020). https://doi.org/10.1007/978-3-030-22441-7

16. Shishkov, B., Larsen, J.B., Warnier, M., Janssen, M.: Three categories of context-aware systems. In: Shishkov, B. (ed.) BMSD 2018. LNBIP, vol. 319, pp. 185–202. Springer, Cham (2018). https://doi.org/10.1007/978-3-319-94214-8_12

17. Shishkov, B., van Sinderen, M.: From user context states to context-aware applications. In: Filipe, J., Cordeiro, J., Cardoso, J. (eds.) ICEIS 2007. LNBIP, vol. 12, pp. 225–239. Springer, Heidelberg (2008). https://doi.org/10.1007/978-3-540-88710-2_18

18. Shishkov, B.: Tuning the behavior of context-aware applications. In: Shishkov, B. (ed.) BMSD 2019. LNBIP, vol. 356, pp. 134–152. Springer, Cham (2019). https://doi.org/10.1007/978-3-030-24854-3_9

19. Han, J., Kamber, M., Pei, J.: Data Mining: Concepts and Techniques, 3rd edn. Morgan Kaufmann Publ. Inc., San Francisco (2011)

20. Dietz, J.L.G.: Enterprise Ontology, Theory and Methodology. Springer, Heidelberg (2006). https://doi.org/10.1007/3-540-33149-2

21. Bunge, M.A.: Treatise on Basic Philosophy. A World of Systems, vol. 4. D. Reidel Publishing Company, Dordrecht (1979)

22. Shishkov, B., Mendling, J.: Business process variability and public values. In: Shishkov, B. (ed.) BMSD 2018. LNBIP, vol. 319, pp. 401–411. Springer, Cham (2018). https://doi.org/10.1007/978-3-319-94214-8_31

23. van Veenstra, A.F., Janssen, M., Tan, Y.H.: Towards an understanding of E-government induced change – drawing on organization and structuration theories. In: Wimmer, M.A., Chappelet, J.L., Janssen, M., Scholl, H.J. (eds.) EGOV 2010. LNCS, vol. 6228, pp. 1–12. Springer, Heidelberg (2010). https://doi.org/10.1007/978-3-642-14799-9_1

24. Bordini, R.H., Fisher, M., Wooldridge, M., Visser, W.: Model checking rational agents. IEEE Intell. Syst. **19**(5), 46–52 (2004)

25. Dey, A., Abowd, G., Salber, D.: A conceptual framework and a toolkit for supporting the rapid prototyping of context-aware applications. Hum. Comput. Interact. **16**(2), 97–166 (2001)

26. Silvander, J.: On context frames and their implementations. In: Shishkov, B. (ed.) BMSD 2021. LNBIP, vol. 422, pp. 133–153. Springer, Cham (2021). https://doi.org/10.1007/978-3-030-79976-2_8

27. Dey, A.K., Newberger, A.: Support for context-aware intelligibility and control. In: Proceedings of the SIGCHI Conference on Human Factors in Computing Systems. ACM, USA (2009)

28. Bosems, S., van Sinderen, M.: Models in the design of context-aware well-being applications. In: Meersman, R., et al. (eds.) OTM 2014. LNCS, vol. 8842, pp. 37–42. Springer, Heidelberg (2014). https://doi.org/10.1007/978-3-662-45550-0_6

29. Alegre, U., Augusto, J.C., Clark, T.: Engineering context-aware systems and applications. J. Syst. Softw. 117(C), 55–83 (2016)
30. Alférez, G.H., Pelechano, V.: Context-aware autonomous web services in software product lines. Proceedings of the 15th International SPLC Conference, CA, USA. IEEE (2011)
31. Abeywickrama, D.B., Ramakrishnan, S.: Context-aware services engineering: models, transformations, and verification. ACM Trans. Internet Technol. J. 11(3), Article 10 (2012)
32. Schilit, B., Adams, N., Want, R.: Context-aware computing applications. In: First Workshop on Mobile Computing Systems and Applications, pp. 85–90. IEEE (1994)
33. Harter, A., Hopper, A., Steggles, P., Ward, A., Webster, P.: The anatomy of a context-aware application. Wirel. Netw. 8, 187–197 (2002)
34. Dey, A.K.: Context-aware computing: the CyberDesk project. In: AAAI Spring Symposium on Intelligent Environments, AAAI Technical Report SS-88-02, pp. 51–54 (1998)
35. Abecker, A., Bernardi, A., Hinkelmann, K., et al.: Context-aware, proactive delivery of task-specific information: the KnowMore project. Inf. Syst. Front. 2, 253–276 (2000)
36. van Sinderen, M., van Halteren, A., Wegdam, M., et al.: Supporting context-aware mobile applications: an infrastructure approach. IEEE Commun. Mag. 44(9), 96–104 (2006)
37. Chaari, T., Laforest, F., Celentano, A.: Adaptation in context-aware pervasive information systems: the SECAS project. Int. J. Pervasive Comput. Commun. 3(4), 400–425 (2007)
38. Pawar, P., Van Beijnum, B., Hermens, H., Konstantas, D.: Analysis of context-aware network selection schemes for power savings. In: Proceedings of the Asia-Pacific Services Computing Conference, pp. 587–594. IEEE (2008)
39. Van Engelenburg, S.: Designing context-aware architectures for business-to-government information sharing. Ph.D. thesis. TU Delft Press (2019)
40. Wegdam, M.: AWARENESS: a project on context AWARE mobile NEtworks and ServiceS. In: Proceedings of the 14th Mobile & Wireless Communications Summit. EURASIP (2005)
41. Levin, R.I., Rubin, D.S.: Statistics for Management. Prentice Hall, Englewood Cliffs (1997)
42. Wasserman, T., Wasserman, L.: Motivation, effort, and neural network modeling: implications. In: Wasserman, T., Wasserman, L. (eds.) Motivation, Effort, and the Neural Network Model. NNMAI, pp. 145–160. Springer, Cham (2020). https://doi.org/10.1007/978-3-030-58724-6_12
43. Hristea, F.T.: The Naïve Bayes Model for Unsupervised Word sense Disambiguation. SpringerBriefs in Statistics. Springer, Heidelberg (2013). https://doi.org/10.1007/978-3-642-33693-5

# The Societal Impacts of Drones: A Public Values Perspective

Boris Shishkov[1,2,3（✉）] and Magdalena Garvanova[2]

[1] Institute of Mathematics and Informatics, Bulgarian Academy of Sciences, Sofia, Bulgaria
[2] Faculty of Information Sciences, University of Library Studies and Information Technologies, Sofia, Bulgaria
m.garvanova@unibit.bg
[3] Institute IICREST, Sofia, Bulgaria
b.b.shishkov@iicrest.org

**Abstract.** Drones appear to be helpful in replacing people and/or providing services to people: this is when operating in dangerous environments, when overcoming distances (both horizontally and vertically), and so on. Nevertheless, it remains insufficiently clear how drone missions could be usefully facilitated by capabilities of guaranteeing against the violation of public values, such as safety, privacy, and accountability. In the current position paper, we refer to literature and previous work for the topics of drone technology and public values, presenting on top of that views that concern mitigations when such values have been violated. Reflecting this in corresponding technical architectures and validating them accordingly is left for future work.

**Keywords:** Drone technology · Public values · Mitigation

## 1 Introduction

*Unmanned Aerial Vehicles* (*UAV*), or *"drones"*, appear to offer a flexible, accurate and affordable solution to many current technical and societal challenges [1]. As studied in another paper of the current proceedings [2]: Drones are not only capable of *replacing people in dangerous environments* and can make use of *advanced sensing capabilities* allowing for *situational awareness*, but they are also *available in different sizes* – small ones can reach difficult to access places; larger drones can monitor buildings, cities, or regions for many hours in a row. Nevertheless, it remains insufficiently clear how drone missions could be usefully facilitated by capabilities of *guaranteeing against the violation of public values*, such as *safety*, *privacy*, and *accountability* [3, 4].

As studied by Garvanova et al. [5]: ***Public values*** are *desires of the general public, that are about properties considered societally valuable*, such as respecting the privacy of citizens or prohibiting polluting activities. "Translating" *public values* into *functional solutions* is thus an actual challenge. Even though *Value-Sensitive Design* (*VSD*) [6] is about *weaving public values in the design of (technical) systems*, it stays

© The Author(s), under exclusive license to Springer Nature Switzerland AG 2022
B. Shishkov and A. Lazarov (Eds.): ICTRS 2022, CCIS 1730, pp. 61–71, 2022.
https://doi.org/10.1007/978-3-031-23226-8_5

insufficiently concrete as it concerns the alignment between abstract *public values* and *technical solutions*.

Acknowledging the efforts of the *UAV* Community concerning *public values* and their adequate "coverage", we claim that currently it is still widely possible that a drone:

- Bumps into a person/vehicle or falls over a person, or shoots at a person, and so on (=> SAFETY violation(s));
- Photographs faces of people in an unauthorized way, disturbs people by producing noise, frightens people when appearing "out of the blue", and so on (=> PRIVACY violation(s));
- Causes damages and afterwards it is impossible to identify the person responsible for that (=> ACCOUNTABILITY violation(s));
- and so on.

With regard to this, we argue that absolutely ruling out those issues is far from realistic nowadays. Hence, we look towards the goal of achieving relevant *mitigations*, such that the *societal acceptance* of *drone technology* increases.

We refer to *literature* and *previous work* for the topics of *drone technology* and *public values*, presenting on top of that views that concern *mitigations* when such values have been violated.

Reflecting this in corresponding technical architectures and validating them accordingly is left for future work.

The remaining of the current position paper is structured as follows: We briefly discuss drone technology in Sect. 2 and public values – in Sect. 3. In Sect. 4 we present our views. Finally, we conclude the paper in Sect. 5, presenting also our plans for future work.

## 2 Drone Technology – Key Points

In considering drone technology, we refer to [7–18] and with regard to positioning the drone system between societal demands and governance we refer to [19–22]. Further, in line with [2], we view a drone as an *agent* that is *autonomous to some degree and adaptive*; it is *capable of gathering relevant contextual information* by means of *sensing*; and in the end, a drone has the ability of *analyzing this data* (for the sake of *decision making*) by means of *algorithms*. Finally, inspired by all this and considering [1], we are briefly addressing in the current section several key issues as follows: (a) *What are drones*; (b) *What can drones do*; (c) *The societal impact of drones*.

Drones are essentially driven by a corresponding mission and managing the mission is hence crucial. As studied in [2], it is sensitive to the "current" situation that is to be somehow determined by the drone – this is often done by means of sensors. The mission management also concerns the drone's behavior adaptation. Hence, we view drones as **flying pilotless agents** (*underwater drones* [23] are left beyond the scope of this paper, as also suggested by the label "unmanned aerial vehicles") **that are navigated from a ground station/ground operator and driven by a pre-defined mission whose goals they realize by performing context-aware behavior** [24–29] **and data-analytics-driven decision making** [2, 30].

According, to Sandbrook, what drones can do depends on *what they are able to carry* [1]: equipment commonly mounted on drones includes still and video cameras (further subdivided into passively reflected thermal and infrared radiation and emitted thermal radiation sensing devices), audio monitoring devices, loudspeakers, liquid sprayers (e.g. for herbicides), accelerometers, GPS and light emitting devices, and so on. Further, *size* matters as well - whilst large drones can carry heavy equipment, smaller units are capable of carrying only very light devices. Finally, the exclusive usage of drones for military applications is past – currently drones are used in *numerous application domains*: from area monitoring through rescue operations to services concerning disruptive events and border security [8, 9, 31]. Hence, drones are capable of realizing various services, such as: ● taking photos/videos; ● monitoring; ● data collection and transmission; ● transportation/delivery of goods; ● (military) shooting; ● illumination; ● and so on.

With regard to drones' societal relevance, it often concerns some ethical implications and the ways in which they might infringe privacy and civil liberties [32]; as already discussed in the Introduction, violating the privacy (for example) of a person is quite possible, in the context of a drone servicing. Still, affecting a particular person is not exhausting drones' societal relevance (in our view) since safety, accountability, and other relevant issues go beyond the mere violation of civil liberties - we stand for a broader perspective on the societal relevance of drones, covering not only the individual person but also the crowd (a number of persons who appear to be in the same context), the manned vehicles, and the institutions/businesses – see Fig. 1 where the following visualizations are used: ● in the left side we have visualized a drone; ● to the right of it and in the middle of the figure, we have visualized an individual person (up) and a crowd (a number of persons) – down: ● finally, at the right side of the figure, we have visualized vehicles (through images featuring a train, a car, and an airplane) – down, and institutions (through an image featuring an institutional building) – up; ● dashed lines are used (with arrows in both directions) to indicate relationships among persons, crowds, vehicles, and institutions; ● four lines are used (with arrows in one direction) to indicate the (potential) IMPACT of drones with regard to persons, crowds, vehicles, and institutions; ● the dashed lines indicate that what they are featuring goes beyond the direct scope of the current paper unlike what concerns drones.

As the figure suggests:

- Drones have the potential of straightforwardly impacting an individual person, for example: a drone could photograph the face of a person (without a permission), bother a person (by producing noise), scare a person, injure a person, and so on.
- Drones could do similar things to a crowd with even more severe consequences not only because this would affect more persons but also because undesired crowd behaviors might be triggered, such as panic, that in turn may lead to also other negative effects.
- Drones could disturb vehicles by physically bumping into them and/or disturbing their (telecommunication) facilitations, which in turn could affect the safety of people.
- Drones could impact institutions by for example acquiring and distributing photo/video data that may be institutionally-sensitive and hence with the potential of affecting (many) people.

Those issues concern public values that will be addressed in the following section.

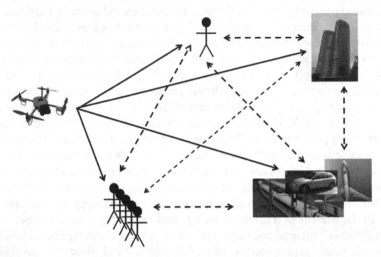

**Fig. 1.** The societal impact of drones

## 3 Public Values

The discussion presented in the current section is mainly inspired by previous work [5] where public values (see Sect. 1) are split in two categories, namely: atomic public values and composite public values. The public values ("values", for short) that were mentioned before, such as safety, privacy, and accountability, are *encapsulating only one particular behavioral goal* – hence, in that sense they are ATOMIC. In contrast, there are values that *reflect a particular human attitude* rather than just a desired behavioral goal – they are COMPOSITE, for example: the desire to achieve egalitarianism [33].

Whereas, *atomic values* are weave-able in a (technical) design, as studied by Shishkov et al. [21, 27, 34], they are claimed to be not very "instrumental" as it concerns social feedback. In our view that is because most of those values (such as *privacy, transparency, accountability*, and so on) are to be considered in a particular context [28, 34] and people consider them differently depending on the context. For example: USUALLY, *privacy* is desired but when HUNTING TERRORISTS, it might be acceptable by many people that authorities compromise their *privacy*. Therefore, studying in general what somebody's attitude is towards *privacy* (for example), would be of limited use. For this reason, we argue that *atomic values could only be adequately operationalized if this concerns context-aware systems* [24–28].

*Composite values* (such as *egalitarianism, utilitarianism, autonomy, embeddedness*, and so on), in contrast, are not so easy to weave in the design (because they are even more abstract than atomic values) but it is easier to capture public opinion concerning them through surveys (or other analyses), as it is claimed by Veenhoven & Kalmijn [35];

they argue that many issues that concern *composite public values can be measured using surveys.*

Hence, *atomic values* can be operationalized but it is not easy justifying this as a public demand; on the other hand, it is not straightforward operationalizing *composite values* but the corresponding *needs* can be "measured".

In considering *composite values* from a *social sciences* perspective, we refer to Shalom Schwartz according to whom every culture can be described by 7 universal *value orientations* (categories), namely: *embeddedness, intellectual autonomy, affective autonomy, hierarchy, egalitarianism, harmony,* and *mastery* [36]:

- *Embeddedness* focuses on maintaining the status quo and limiting the actions and inclinations that can disrupt the solidarity of the group or the imposed traditional order;
- *Intellectual autonomy* expresses the aspirations of individuals to pursue their own ideas and independent intellectual purposes;
- *Affective autonomy* expresses the desire of individuals to acquire affective positive experience;
- *Hierarchy* emphasizes the legitimacy of the unequal distribution of power, roles, and resources;
- *Egalitarianism* reveals the transcendence of individual interests in favor of voluntary commitment and concern for the welfare of others;
- *Harmony* discloses the unity with the environment;
- *Mastery* gives priority to active self-assertion and control of the social and natural environment.

Inspired by the above and referring to previous work [4], we explicitly address the AUTHORITY concept, arguing that it is of particular relevance as it concerns the societal impacts of drones because whatever a drone may "do" (for the *benefit* or *harm* of people) would be rooted in the actual *authority* embedded in the drone and its mission. We have studied how capturing *human authority* can be achieved "through" measuring corresponding *composite values* and an important question is which particular *composite values* to consider. In this regard, we have considered the concept of *power* that is obviously close to the concept of (*human authority*). Then we ask the question: WHAT gives power? In our view, it is more or less three things: (i) the organizational structure; (ii) the broader attitudes; (iii) the behavior models of surrounding persons. In [4], we have reflected (i), (ii), and (iii) in corresponding *bipolar dimensions,* as follows: ● the *hierarchy* vs. *egalitarianism* dimension, featuring (i); ● the *autonomy* vs. *conservatism* (*embeddedness*) dimension, featuring (ii); ● the *harmony* vs. *mastery* dimension, featuring (iii). Relating this to the *human authority* concept ("*authority*", for short) is visualized in Fig. 2:

As the figure suggests, by analyzing *composite values* along those dimensions, is expected to be helpful in getting unbiased perception as it concerns *authority*; then we would know what is SOCIETALLY ACCEPTABLE as it concerns *drone-technology-related designs* and *drone-missions-planning.*

Based on the above discussion, we derive conclusions that are two-fold:

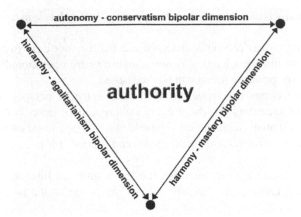

**Fig. 2.** Relating the authority concept to composite values (Source: [4], p. 294 ©2019, Springer, reprinted with permission)

- At STRATEGIC level, designers of drone systems/technologies are to take into account the public opinion that concerns AUTHORITY (in the drone technology context);
- At OPERATIONAL level and restricted by the above, designers must consider as much as possible the relevant *atomic values* and operationalize them accordingly.

Considering further the societal impacts of drones we bridge (in the following section) the discussions carried out in the current and the previous sections.

## 4    Using Drones – Societal Implications: Mitigation Views

We argue that *values violations* are inevitable as it concerns drone operations because all-encompassing algorithms are far from realistic. At the same time, we claim that *mitigation* measures are often possible and could (substantially) "soften" the effects of such violations. This concerns both *Design Time* (*DT*) and *Real-Time* (*RT*) – at DT we may take preventive mitigation actions while at RT we may achieve mitigations, by adapting the drone behavior and/or the usage of generated data. This vision is reflected in Fig. 3. There we use OWL notations [37] to reflect several identified key mitigation action types, clustered accordingly as DT-actions (see the left side of the Figure) vs RT-actions (see the right side of the Figure). The line with label "balance" indicates that DT-actions and RT-actions should be applied in synch; also these actions are to be measurable things, such that we are able to "extract" values that would indicate for corresponding situations (see the upper part of the Figure).

As also seen in the Figure: The DT-actions represent the first cluster (from left to right) covering OPERATIONALIZATIONS (that concern ATOMIC values) and STRATEGIC CONSIDERATIONS (that concern composite values) – see Sect. 3; The RT-actions represent the second cluster (from left to right) covering BEHAVIOR ADAPTATIONS and USABILITY UPDATES. Moreover:

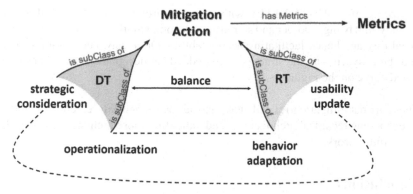

**Fig. 3.** Clustering mitigation actions

- At DT, we may use societal feedback (achieved by means of surveys, for example) concerning composite values and particularly directed towards AUTHORITY-related issues (see Sect. 3), such that we know how to deal with authority-related considerations concerning drone missions in general. This would help building up drone-mission-related STRATEGIES that "draw" the broad DESIGN RESTRICTIONS. Such actions would be mitigation-oriented and preventive in the sense that they would at least "guarantee" against cases of severely unacceptable "behavior" of drones.
- Also at DT, we may take actions on operationalizing ATOMIC VALUES, by specifying solution instances for each anticipated situation class. For example: if persons are identified in close proximity to the drone of consideration and there is no given agreement, the drone system could only do photo/video recordings if blurring all faces, such that PRIVACY is respected.
- At RT, it is possible that a situation pops up, that has not been anticipated at design time and hence a design time value operationalization is not "available". This means that context-awareness [24] is impossible and the drone should follow a "general" behavior line. Still in this it may be possible to identify a SENSITIVE SITUATION PATTERN, as for example: "point of no return reached" (this is "sensitive" because if the drone would not fly back, then there is risk of it crashing over a person or a building and this relates to SAFETY) – there should be general rules covering all such sensitive issues, and in this case it should be: "stop all activities and fly back immediately". The dashed line between *behavior adaptation* and *operationalization* indicates that often adapting drone behavior at real time relates to value operationalizations rooted in the design, and both need to be in synch. For example: If a drone mission assumes taking photos and when approaching people the value operationalization "asks" for blurring faces. Then this all goes in conflict with the instruction: "stop all activities and fly back immediately" (see above). Resolving such "tensions" requires pre-defined value hierarchies and prioritizations – in this case, *safety* is above all and the drone flies back immediately.
- Also at RT: When new societal demands need to be fast addressed while implementing new designs takes more time, then a solution may be to go for real-time updates in how the drone-generated data is used. For example: if huge societal "push" pops up

concerning ACCOUNTABILITY with regard to drone missions, then all incoming data may start being recorder and stored at the Ground Station, for the sake of allowing traceability and hence facilitating accountability. Obviously, such usability updates are to be in synch with the strategies "embedded" at design time, as indicated by the dashed curve on the Figure.

Those are our mitigation-related views and, as mentioned before, reflecting the views in corresponding technical architectures and validating those architectures accordingly is left for future work.

## 5 Conclusions

Drones appear to offer flexible, accurate and affordable solutions to many current technical and societal challenges but at the same time there are societal implications that concern drone usage. This relates to both atomic public values (such as safety, privacy, and accountability) and composite public values (such as conservatism, egalitarianism, and so on). Often, as a result of drone usage, some public values are violated. Is this unavoidable and if yes, what could be done for mitigating such violations?

We have tried to find answers to those questions, referring to literature and previous work touching upon drone technology and public values. On that basis, we have proposed views that concern mitigations when such values have been violated, envisioning design-time mitigation actions and real-time mitigation actions.

We have elaborated our views and partially exemplified our ideas.

We believe that: ● Any value is to be reflected in particular demands/requirements that are of non-functional essence and in order to adequately consider them, they need to be reflected in corresponding functional solutions that concern the drone system design. ● Composite public values should be given higher priority to atomic public values because the former concern wider Society while the latter would most often concern the needs/interests of a particular individual. ● Within each category, public values are to be organized in hierarchies, suggesting higher priority to those values that are about human life (such as safety, for example), as opposed to values, such as privacy and accountability, for example.

Reflecting this in the proposal and validation of corresponding technical architectures is left for future work.

**Acknowledgement.** This work is supported by the Bulgarian National Science Fund, project title "Synthesis of a dynamic model for assessing the psychological and physical impacts of excessive use of smart technologies", KP-06-N 32/4/07.12.2019.

# References

1. Sandbrook, C.: The social implications of using drones for biodiversity conservation. Ambio **44**(Suppl 4), 636–647 (2015)
2. Shishkov, B., Ivanova, K., Verbraeck, A., Van Sinderen, M.: Combining context-awareness and data analytics in support of drone technology. In: Shishkov, B., Lazarov, A. (eds.) Telecommunications and Remote Sensing. ICTRS 2022. Communications in Computer and Inf. Science, vol. 1730. Springer, Cham (2022)
3. Shishkov, B., Hristozov, S., Janssen, M., Van den Hoven, J.: Drones in land border missions: benefits and accountability concerns. In Proceedings of the 6th International Conference on Telecommunications and Remote Sensing (ICTRS 2017). ACM, New York, NY, USA (2017)
4. Garvanova, M., Shishkov, B.: Capturing human authority and responsibility by considering composite public values. In: Shishkov, B. (ed.) Business Modeling and Software Design. BMSD 2019. Lecture Notes in Business Information Processing, vol. 356, pp. 290–298 Springer, Cham (2019). https://doi.org/10.1007/978-3-030-24854-3_22
5. Garvanova, M., Shishkov, B., Janssen, M.: Composite public values and software specifications. In: Shishkov, B. (ed.) Business Modeling and Software Design. BMSD 2018. Lecture Notes in Business Information Processing, vol. 319, pp. 412–420. Springer, Cham (2018). https://doi.org/10.1007/978-3-319-94214-8_32
6. Friedman, B., Hendry, D.G., Borning, A.: A survey of value sensitive design methods. Found. Trends, p. 76 (2017)
7. Griffin, G.F.: The use of unmanned aerial vehicles for disaster management. Geomatica **68**(4), 265–281 (2014)
8. Shishkov, B., Branzov, T., Ivanova, K., Verbraeck, A.: Using drones for resilience: a system of systems perspective. In: Proceedings of 10th International Conference on Telecommunications and Remote Sensing (ICTRS 2021). Association for Computing Machinery, New York, NY, USA (2021)
9. Shishkov, B., Hristozov, S., Verbraeck, A.: Improving resilience using drones for effective monitoring after disruptive events. In: Proceedings of 9th International Conference on Telecommunications and Remote Sensing (ICTRS 2020). Association for Computing Machinery, New York, NY, USA (2020)
10. Martini, T., Lynch, M., Weaver, A., van Vuuren, T.: The humanitarian use of drones as an emerging technology for emerging needs. In: Custers, B. (ed.) The Future of Drone Use. Information Technology and Law Series, vol. 27. T.M.C. Asser Press, The Hague (2016). https://doi.org/10.1007/978-94-6265-132-6_7
11. Milas, A.S., Cracknell, A.P., Warner, T.A.: Drones – the third generation source of remote sensing data. Int. J. Remote Sens. **39**(21), 7125–7137 (2018)
12. Kayan, H., Eslampanah, R., Yeganli, F., Askar, M.: Heat leakage detection and surveillance using aerial thermography drone. In: Proceedings of 26th Signal Processing and Communications Applications Conference (SIU) (2018)
13. Pandey, S., Barik, R.K., Gupta, S., Arthi, R.: Pandemic Drone with Thermal Imaging and Crowd Monitoring System (DRISHYA). In: Tripathy, H.K., Mishra, S., Mallick, P.K., Panda, A.R. (eds.) Technical Advancements of Machine Learning in Healthcare. SCI, vol. 936, pp. 307–325. Springer, Singapore (2021). https://doi.org/10.1007/978-981-33-4698-7_15
14. Hill, A.C., Laugier, E.J., Casana, J.: Archaeological remote sensing using multi-temporal, drone-acquired thermal and near infrared (NIR) imagery: a case study at the Enfield Shaker Village, New Hampshire. Remote Sens. 12(4), 690 (2020)
15. Carrio, A., Sampedro, C., Rodriguez-Ramos, A., Campoy, P.: A review of deep learning methods and applications for unmanned aerial vehicles. J. Sens. vol. 2017, Article ID 3296874 (2017)

16. Erdelj, M., Natalizio, E., Chowdhury, K.R., Akyildiz, I.F.: Help from the sky: leveraging UAVs for disaster management. IEEE Pervasive Comput. **16**(1), 24–32 (2017)
17. Kopardekar, P., Rios, J., Prevot, Th., Johnson, M., Jung, J., Robinson III, J.E.: Unmanned aircraft system traffic management (UTM) concept of operations. In: Proceedings of the 16th AIAA Aviation Technology, Integration, and Operations Conference, Washington, D.C., USA (2016)
18. American red cross drones for disaster response and relief operations (2015). https://www.issuelab.org/resources/21683/21683.pdf
19. Dietz, J.L.G.: Enterprise Ontology, Theory and Methodology. Springer, Heidelberg (2006)
20. Bunge, M.A.: Treatise on Basic Philosophy. A World of Systems, vol. 4. D. Reidel Publishing Company, Dordrecht (1979)
21. Shishkov, B., Mendling, J.: Business process variability and public values. In: Shishkov B. (ed.) Business Modeling and Software Design. BMSD 2018. Lecture Notes in Business Information Processing, vol. 319, pp. 401–411. Springer, Cham (2018). https://doi.org/10.1007/978-3-319-94214-8_31
22. van Veenstra, A.F., Janssen, M., Tan, Y.H.: Towards an understanding of E-Government induced change – drawing on organization and structuration theories. In: Wimmer, M.A., Chappelet, J.L., Janssen, M., Scholl, H.J. (eds.) Electronic Government. EGOV 2010. Lecture Notes in Computer Science, vol. 6228, pp. 1–12. Springer, Heidelberg (2010). https://doi.org/10.1007/978-3-642-14799-9_1
23. Yar, G.N.A.H., Ahmad, A., Khurshid, K.: Low cost assembly design of unmanned underwater vehicle (UUV). In: International Bhurban Conference on Applied Sciences and Technologies (IBCAST), pp. 829–834. IEEE (2021)
24. Shishkov, B., van Sinderen, M.: Towards well-founded and richer context-awareness conceptual models. In: Shishkov, B. (ed.) Business Modeling and Software Design. BMSD 2021. Lecture Notes in Business Information Processing, vol. 422, pp. 118–132. Springer, Cham (2021). https://doi.org/10.1007/978-3-030-79976-2_7
25. Shishkov, B., van Sinderen, M.: On the context-aware servicing of user needs: extracting and managing context information supported by rules and predictions. In: Shishkov, B. (ed.) Business Modeling and Software Design. BMSD 2022. LNBIP, vol. 453, pp. 240–248. Springer, Cham (2022). https://doi.org/10.1007/978-3-031-11510-3_15
26. Shishkov, B.: Designing Enterprise Information Systems, Merging Enterprise Modeling and Software Specification. Springer, Cham (2020)
27. Shishkov, B., Larsen, J.B., Warnier, M., Janssen, M.: Three categories of context-aware systems. In: Shishkov B. (ed.) Business Modeling and Software Design. BMSD 2018. Lecture Notes in Business Information Processing, vol. 319, pp. 185–202. Springer, Cham (2018). https://doi.org/10.1007/978-3-319-94214-8_12
28. Shishkov, B., van Sinderen, M.: From user context states to context-aware applications. In: Filipe, J., Cordeiro, J., Cardoso, J. (eds.) Enterprise Information Systems. ICEIS 2007. LNBIP, vol. 12, pp. 225–239. Springer, Heidelberg (2008). https://doi.org/10.1007/978-3-540-88710-2_18
29. Shishkov, B.: Tuning the behavior of context-aware applications. In: Shishkov B. (ed.) Business Modeling and Software Design. BMSD 2019. Lecture Notes in Business Information Processing, vol. 356, pp. 134–152. Springer, Cham (2019). https://doi.org/10.1007/978-3-030-24854-3_9
30. Han, J., Kamber, M., Pei, J.: Data Mining: Concepts and Techniques, 3rd edn. Morgan Kaufmann Publ. Inc., San Francisco, CA, USA (2011)
31. Shishkov, B., Mitrakos, D.: Towards context-aware border security control. In: Proceedings of the 6th international symposium on business modeling and software design (BMSD), 20–22 June 2016. SCITEPRESS, Rhodes, Greece (2016)

32. Sparrow, R.: Building a better warbot: ethical issues in the design of unmanned systems for military applications. Sci. Eng. Ethics **15**, 169–187 (2009)
33. Branzei, R., Dimitrov, D., Tijs, S.: Egalitarianism-based solution concepts. Models Coop. Game Theory, 37–42. Springer, Berlin, Heidelberg (2008)
34. Shishkov, B., Janssen, M.: Enforcing context-awareness and privacy-by-design in the specification of information systems. In: Shishkov B. (ed.) Business Modeling and Software Design. BMSD 2017. Lecture Notes in Business Information Processing, vol. 309, pp. 87–111. Springer, Cham (2018). https://doi.org/10.1007/978-3-319-78428-1_5
35. Veenhoven, R., Kalmijn, W.J.: Inequality-adjusted happiness in nations egalitarianism and utilitarianism married in a new index of societal performance. J. Happiness Stud. vol. 6(4), 421–455. Springer (2005)
36. Schwartz, S.H.: The Refined Theory of Basic Values. In: Roccas, S., Sagiv, L. (eds.) Values and Behavior, pp. 51–72. Springer, Cham (2017). https://doi.org/10.1007/978-3-319-56352-7_3
37. OWL (2022). https://www.w3.org/OWL

# Studying the Impact of PV Plants on Power Quality

Radoslav Simionov(✉), Ginko Georgiev, Kamen Seymenliyski, Radostin Dolchinkov, Silvia Letskovska, Eldar Zaerov, Atanas Yovkov, and Nikolina Dragneva

Faculty of Computer Science and Engineering, Burgas Free University, Burgas, Bulgaria
radoslav.simionov@gmail.com, {ggeorgiev,kdimitrov,rado,silvia, dragneva}@bfu.bg

**Abstract.** World experience in the field of renewable energy shows an increase in efficiency in the generation of clean energy as a result of the use of small production power plants (micro-plants), meeting the energy needs of individual consumers in the residential sector, as well as small production enterprises.

The composition of these power plants includes not only photovoltaic modules, but also a series of power electronic devices, acting as an interface between them and the electrical network, aiming to achieve the efficient use of available solar energy.

The performance of photovoltaic power plants depends on many factors, such as location, climatic conditions, mechanical losses, etc. The price of the electricity produced by them, however, significantly depends on the possibilities of their inclusion in the general energy network.

**Keywords:** PV central · Production of electric energy · Productivity · Smart cities

## 1 Introduction

Climate change is the greatest challenge of our time. The deterioration of the environment is a threat to the very existence of Europe and the world.

As a result of our increased dependence on energy and scarce energy resources, there is a trend towards accelerated construction of new capacities from renewable energy sources. This process helps reduce greenhouse gas emissions, therefore contributing to mitigating the effects of climate change, which is the goal of the "green transition" [1–5].

The mass deployment of photovoltaic power generation systems that are not built and managed efficiently also causes a number of negative effects [6–8].

Part of these negative effects are expressed in an unfavorable influence on the quality of the electricity that is supplied to consumers close to the source of renewable energy.

This report examines the adverse impact of variations in electricity generation from photovoltaic plants caused by seasonal, climatic and hourly factors on the shape of voltage and current supplying consumers.

© The Author(s), under exclusive license to Springer Nature Switzerland AG 2022
B. Shishkov and A. Lazarov (Eds.): ICTRS 2022, CCIS 1730, pp. 72–84, 2022.
https://doi.org/10.1007/978-3-031-23226-8_6

The study of these adverse phenomena increases the possibilities for compensating these harmful influences on consumers and increasing the energy efficiency of hybrid systems for the production and consumption of "green" electricity obtained from photovoltaic plants of different power. The obtained results enable the passage and development of smart cities.

## 2 Development of Technologies Related to RES

In the last fifteen years, renewable energy technologies have been actively developed, in particular - the production of electricity from the sun and wind.

Globally, the share of photovoltaic capacities is within 1.1%. The exponential increase in the installed capacity of photovoltaic systems, which began in 2000, reached in 2015 values of the order of 50 GW.

At the end of 2018, the installed capacity of photovoltaic plants in the world was on the order of 500 GW.

The factor that led to this rapid development of solar energy is the sharp reduction in the price of photovoltaic modules. As a result, the cost of energy produced by this type of plant has also significantly decreased.

It is assumed that in the next 10–20 years, a reduction in the price and technical equipment included in the photovoltaic power plants can be expected, by 2025 - of the order of 59%.

The price of lead-acid and lithium-ion batteries is expected to decrease by 48% and 58% by 2030, respectively.

World experience in the field of renewable energy shows an increase in efficiency in the generation of clean energy as a result of the use of small production power plants (micro-plants), meeting the energy needs of individual consumers in the residential sector, as well as small production enterprises.

The composition of these power plants includes not only photovoltaic modules, but also a series of power electronic devices, acting as an interface between them and the electrical network, aiming to achieve the efficient use of available solar energy.

The performance of photovoltaic power plants depends on many factors, such as location, climatic conditions, mechanical losses, etc. The price of the electricity produced by them, however, significantly depends on the possibilities of their inclusion in the general energy network [9–13].

By plugging into this grid, small power plants can operate without the need to install expensive energy accumulators and sell the excess electricity produced to other consumers. Thus, the return on investment of such systems turns out to be much shorter than that of autonomous energy supply systems.

The inclusion in the general network of many small power plants with non-constant electricity generation leads to the need for a significant technical modernization of the technical systems [14–16].

Micro power plants for the production of electrical energy are systems located directly at the energy consumer with the possibility of self-consumption of the produced energy, sale of excess electricity in the network and purchase of energy in case of insufficient production.

This is a priority direction in the development of solar energy, a major factor for the future increase in the percentage of RES-based power plants in the general structure of generating capacities and transformations in the modern electricity industry.

The part of locally consumed energy from the total generated by the micro power plants is characterized by the so-called self-consumption rate.

The coefficient of self-consumption is equal to the ratio of the amount of generated energy consumed locally to the amount of the total volume of energy generated by the photovoltaic modules [17–19].

The coefficient actually shows to what extent the local generation satisfies the energy needs of the user.

The experience of countries that are leaders in the development of renewable energy, such as Germany, the Netherlands, Canada, China, shows that these countries are increasingly using the direct stimulation of micro-generation (micro-power plants) based on the use of renewable energy sources.

This incentive includes feed-in-tariffs, grants and subsidies, as well as tax breaks.

Bonus tariffs make it possible to reduce the repayment period of the equipment, but not the initial capital required to build the micro-plants.

Tax breaks can lead to both a reduction in the initial capital required and a shorter payback period for the equipment.

At the same time, other countries, such as Belgium, the USA and Japan, complement the measures to stimulate the construction of micro-plants based on RES with the creation of local or regional carbon markets.

One of the innovations used in the US by large electricity producers and distributors allows them to provide the necessary indicators by volume of generated renewable energy through the Net Metering scheme.

This scheme allows customers to offset their electricity consumption with energy produced by their own small generating devices (photovoltaic panels or small wind turbines) connected to the public grid [6, 20–24].

At the same time, the measuring electricity meters must measure both in the forward direction (when consuming electricity from the grid) and in the opposite direction (when supplying electricity to the grid), thus enabling the user to measure the electricity produced and given to the grid.

A relatively new measure to stimulate micro-generation of electricity in the US is the "virtual electricity meter" scheme. It allows to obtain a profit from micro-generation of solar energy even by those homeowners who are not able to install photovoltaic panels directly on their own roof, due to shading or for other reasons.

The cost of the energy produced by the photovoltaic system, established on a common roof and/or on other sections of the building structure, is distributed among the residents, in proportion to their share of ownership.

Residents of multi-family buildings can also receive solar power from a nearby micro-generation source of electricity outside their property boundaries, and in some cases, even acquire title to it.

The process of connection to the general distribution network of the micro-generation systems is strictly regulated.

The world experience for state stimulation of micro-generation of electricity and for standardizing the procedures for inclusion in the general distribution network can be considered in the following sequence:

- The microgeneration of renewable energy refers to generating systems with an installed capacity of up to 30 kW;
- When using micro-photovoltaic systems in multi-family buildings, it is possible to work according to the "virtual electricity meter" scheme;
- Measures are planned for financial stimulation of the development of the microgeneration of electricity from RES, in particular - for individuals;

The use of RES is recognized as an ecological and/or energy-saving activity for natural persons carrying out activities in the field of the use of RES.

With decision No. II-17 of 01.07.2019, the Commission for Energy and Water Regulation adopted the general principles for determining preferential prices for electricity produced from renewable sources:

- Amount of investment costs, including the costs of connecting to the relevant transmission or distribution networks;
- Level of operating costs;
- Depreciation costs determined on the basis of the average useful technical-economic life of the assets and returns.

The data from the official report of the Fraunhofer Institute as of the end of March 2019 - Fraunhofer Institute for Solar Energy Systems were used to determine the prices of electricity produced from renewable sources.

From the analysis made in the report of the Fraunhofer institute for Solar energy systems - ISE, it is clear that the investment costs for small rooftop photovoltaic plants from 5 kWp to 30 kWp are in the range of 1200 to 1400 euros/kWp.

Based on the above, it could be assumed that FTPP with a total installed capacity of up to 30 kWp inclusive, which are planned to be built on roof and facade structures of buildings connected to the electricity distribution network and on real estates attached to them in urbanized areas, should be separated in two power ranges.

The first group has a total installed power of up to 5 kWp with investment costs of 1400 euros/kWp, and the second group has a total installed power of more than 5 kWp, up to 30 kWp, with investment costs of 1200 euros/kWp.

A comparison of experimental results from PVGIS (Photovoltaic Geographical Information System), NASA (National Aeronautics and Space Administration), METEONORM and the Bulgarian Academy of Sciences (BAS) for the average annual summary was taken into account when determining the average annual productivity of the FTPP radiation for the city of Varna on a horizontal surface for 2011.

For Bulgaria, average annual total solar radiation has been established from 1210 $kWh/m^2/y$ to 1400 $kWh/m^2/y$ on a horizontal surface.

With an optimal tilt of the photovoltaic panels of $32 \div 33°$, the average annual total solar radiation is from 1366 kWh/y to 1660 $kWh/m^2/y$.

Art. 147. (1) (Supp. - SG No. 65 of 2003) indicates that approval of investment projects is not required for issuing a building permit for (new - SG No. 35 of 2011, in effective from 03.05.2011, amended - SG No. 41 from 2019, effective from 21.05.2019) installation of installations for the production of electrical energy, thermal energy and/or energy for cooling from renewable sources with a total installed capacity of up to 1 MW, including to the existing buildings in the urbanized territories, including on their roof and facade structures and in their adjacent land properties.

The technology for construction and commissioning of the micro-photovoltaic plants follows the algorithm shown in Fig. 4.

Preferential prices for the production of electric energy from renewable sources do not take into account specific values of an individual investment project, but averaged ones taken from official sources and reflecting international experience, as well as acquired and developed experience in the country.

The technical and economic parameters that influence the price of electricity produced by photovoltaic plants, built on roof and facade structures of buildings connected to the electricity distribution network and on real estates attached to them in urbanized areas are the following:

1. Investment costs per kWp in the amount of:

   - BGN 2,738/kWp for photovoltaic plants with a total installed capacity of up to 5 kWp inclusive;
   - BGN 2,347/kWp for photovoltaic plants with a total installed capacity of over 5 kWp up to 30 kWp.

2. Operating costs – environmental protection costs, materials and other costs related to the production process, in the amount of:

   - BGN 71.34/MWh for photovoltaic plants with a total installed capacity of up to 5 kWp inclusive;
   - BGN 54.34/MWh for photovoltaic plants with a total installed capacity of over 5 kWp to 30 kWp.

3. Useful life of assets – 20 years;
4. Inflation of operating costs - 2%;
5. Average annual duration of operation of the plant 1320 h, which equals 1320 kWh/kWp net specific production;
6. Weighted average rate of return – 7%.

After researching the productivity of many micro-PV plants built in Bulgaria, it was found that it varies between 40 ÷ 80% in the maximum (peak) production areas.

The idea of stimulating the connection process of PV plants is to increase the efficiency of electricity generation and reduce transmission losses by building them close to the consumers.

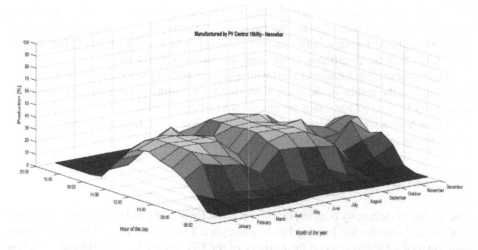

**Fig. 1.** Performance of a PV plant – 16 kWp

However, research shows that the results obtained are not encouraging, due to the following reasons.

The first reason is related to the impossibility of complying with the technological requirements for the construction of such type of plants.

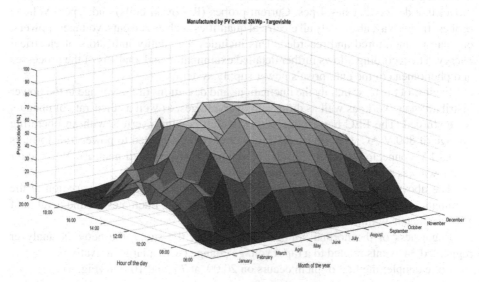

**Fig. 2.** Performance of a PV plant – 30 kWp

The second reason is related to the observed tendency to build these plants in remote areas, with low cost of real estate, but having a small consumption of electrical energy.

Data on the performance of two micro-PV-plants with the same type of photovoltaic panels, but built under different conditions, are shown in Fig. 1 and Fig. 2.

The two plants are located in areas with approximately the same annual average solar radiation, but the results of the study show that the maximum performance of the plant shown in Fig. 5, is 37.88%, and the one shown in Fig. 6 – 79%.

The other round of problems is related to the influence of these plants on the quality of electricity in the supply network.

## 3   Grid Loss

The quality of electricity is an important condition for the safe and trouble-free operation of electrical consumers. The need to conduct such a study was caused by the episodic shutdown of solar inverters on the territory of the FPP - the village of Drazhevo. When the production of electricity from one of the solar inverters stops, a "Grid loss" error is displayed. After falling into the "error" mode, communication with this inverter is lost and this stops the operation of the others as well. A restart is required to resume power generation.

The research was conducted between 19.09.2022 and 22.09.2022 and lasted 2 days, 20 h, 13 min, 53 s, 750 ms on the territory of the FEC - the village of Drazhevo with a network analyzer FLUKE 435 - II, serial number: 34633113. This network analyzer model is a device that has 4 pcs. Current probes (Rogovski coils) and 5 pcs. Voltage probes. In this way, absolutely all electrical quantities such as currents, voltages, powers, etc. can be monitored and recorded. This includes the quality indicators of electrical energy. The recording allows further detailed examination and analysis of the processes and phenomena in the enterprise's power supply system.

In view of the task, mainly the fluctuations and deviations of the voltage in the power distribution network, as well as drops and overvoltages, as well as their rate of change, were studied. The FEC has a large power, which is why inverters with an operating voltage of 800 V AC were selected. The inverters are connected to power transformers 20/0.8 kV connected according to the IT scheme (with isolated neutral). No inverter shutdown was recorded during the study.

The above figure shows a sample of the test showing the voltage variation at the terminals of Transformer 1. It can be seen that the voltage fluctuates around a value of 830 V which is within the permissible limits.

Regardless of the normal voltage values during the study, the network analyzer registered 34 events related to a rapid voltage change (with a large derivative).

For example: the first of them occurs on 20.09. at 7 h and 10 min (Fig. 3) .

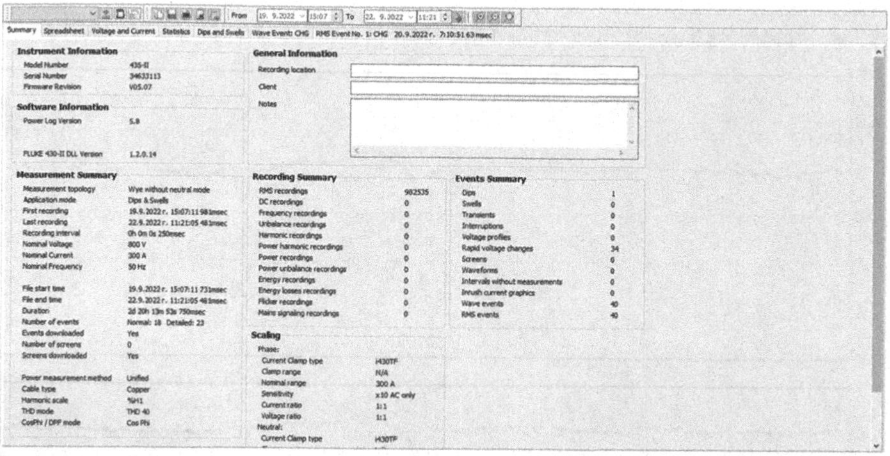

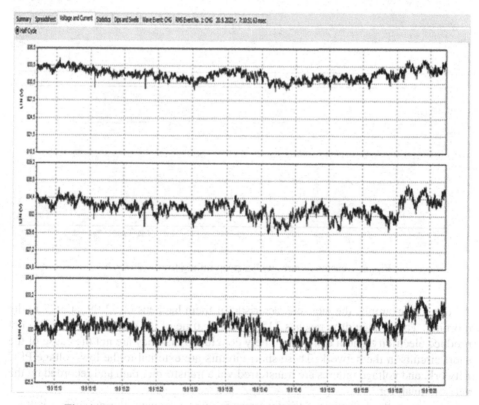

**Fig. 3.** Set parameters on a FLUKE 435 network analyzer

**Fig. 4.** The examination of the voltage at the terminals of a Transformer

Analysis of the records shows that these are voltage failures with a steep falling front. These failures are external to the FEC and occur absolutely randomly, at any time of

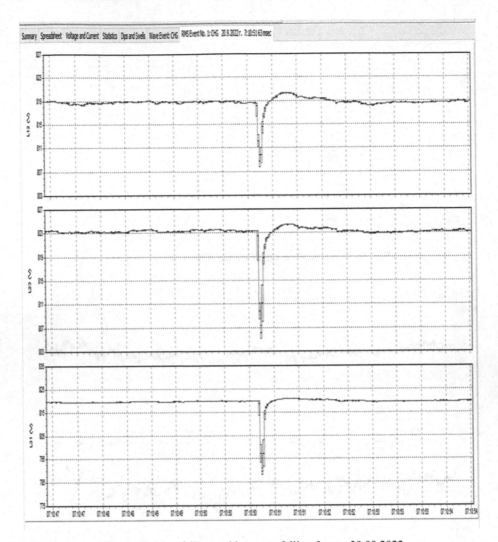

**Fig. 5.** Tension failures with a steep falling front – 20.09.2022

the day. For example, the most characteristic of them happens on 21.09. at 3:27 in the morning. The voltage drop reaches 715 V. At this time of the day, the inverters do not produce electricity, and it can be definitely concluded that they are not the cause of the short circuits in the network. These short-circuits are external to the low-voltage PEC network, and voltage failures are transferred via a transformer path and recorded by the network analyzer.

Moreover, the behavior of the inverters is quite adequate, during such a voltage failure they remain with a higher voltage than the grid and at that moment their current increases, as can be seen from the next record (Fig. 7).

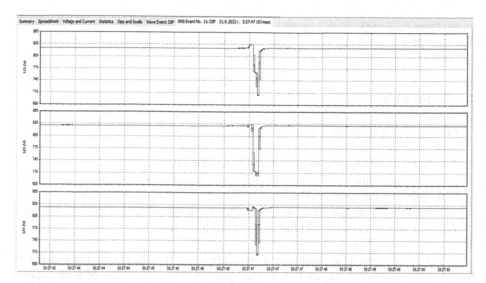

**Fig. 6.** Tension failures with a steep falling front – 21.09.2022

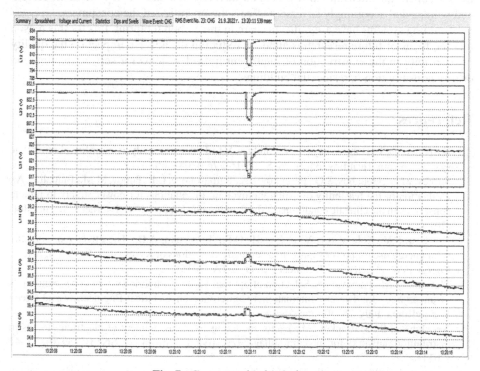

**Fig. 7.** Current and voltage changes

The recording was made on 21.09. at 1:20 p.m. The upper three graphs show the mains voltages, and the lower three the currents of an inverter with number 4 from transformer 1. It works with a current of about 40A. After the occurrence of the event, it is seen how the inverter currents increase and how they recover after the voltage is restored.

## 4   Conclusions

From the analysis of the data from the records, the following conclusions can be drawn:

1. No shutdown of the inverters was registered during the recordings.
2. The Medium Voltage (MV) network of EVN is unstable. Stress failures with a steep falling front are clearly visible.
3. If these failures are deeper or longer due to the adequate response of the inverters (current injection) they could fall into a "Grid loss" state.

All these phenomena are manifested especially strongly when powering consumers from hybrid renewable sources in building systems. The connection of such sources in parallel to the existing building energy system supplying consumers with a different mode of operation intensifies the effect of the adverse influence on the form of the current and voltage and accordingly adversely affects the operation of the consumers.

Building systems have a significant share in the carbon footprint. It is for this reason that the focus of future research is aimed at reducing the adverse impact on the quality of electricity in the construction of intelligent hybrid systems for self-production and energy consumption in residential buildings.

## References

1. Karpenko, D.S., Dubrovskaya, V.V., Shklyar, V.I.: Efficiency analysis of utility photovoltaic systems,. Prom. Heat Eng. **38**(2), 76–80 (2016). 76 0204–3602
2. Surkov, M.A., Obukhov, S.G., Plotnikov, I.A., Sumarokova, L.P., Popov, M.M., Baidali, S.A.: Evaluation of the feasibility of using photovoltaic installations for power supply to remote consumers in the climatic conditions of the Russian north federations. Internet J. Science 8(4) (2016)
3. Kiseleva, S.V., Kolomietc1, Y.G., Popel1, O.S., Tarasenko, A.B.: The effectiveness of the solar energy use for power supply in the climatic conditions of Kyrgyzstan. Int. Sci. J. Altern. Energy Ecol. © Scientific Technical Center TATA (2015)
4. Matsankov, M., Ivanova, M.: Selection of optimal variant of hybrid system under conditions of uncertainty. In: The 2nd International Conference on Electrical Engineering and Green EnergyRoma, Italy, 28–30 June 2019
5. Nedelcheva, S., Matsankov, M.: Factor modeling in the assessment of electricity losses in distribution networks for medium voltage. Izvestiya TU-Sliven **3**(ISSN1312-3920), 37–42 (2011)
6. Vasileva, E., Matsankov, M.: Defining the undelivered energy when exploitation of decentralized energy sources. ICTTE, Yambol (2017). ISSN 1314–9474

7. Bobyl, A.V., Zabrodskii, A.G., Kudryashov, S.A., Malyshkin, V.G., Makarov, V.M., Terukova, E.E., Erk, A.F.: Renormalized model for solar power plants economic efficiency evaluation, Izvestiya Akademii Nauk, Energy, No. 6 (2017)

8. Gabderakhmanova, T.S.: LB Director, Analysis of autonomous power supply schemes based on renewable sources of energy//Promyshlennaya energetika, 4, 48–51 (2015)

9. Varbov, T.K.: Some specific problems with photovoltaic systems connected to the electricity distribution network, Author's abstract of a dissertation for awarding the educational and scientific degree "DOCTOR", Gabrovo, (2015)

10. Energy Development Forecast for Peace and Russia In: 2019 Makarova, A.A, Mitrovoi, T.A., Kulagina, V.A. INEI RAN–Moscow School of Management Skolkovo – Moscow, 2019. – 210 pp. - ISBN 978–5–91438–028–8

11. Ratner, S.V., Aksyuk, T.D.: Foreign experience of stimulating microgenerations based on renewable energy sources: organizational and economic aspects, Scientific and technical reports of SPbGPU. Econ. Sci. 10(4) (2017)

12. Regulation No. 6 of February 24, 2014 on the connection of producers and customers of electricity to the transmission or distribution grids, which is in force since April 4 (2014)

13. Production of electricity with RES & CHP for homeowner, PERCH, guide for home owners. http://www.unicad.bg/pv_kit_home_wkd.htm

14. Innovations in solar inverters, Sp. energy review - issue 6, (2017). https://www.energy-rev iew.bg/bg/inovacii-pri-solarnite-invertori/2/881/

15. Dimitrov, D., Iliev, A.: Decentralized energy production from rooftop photovoltaic systems. Investment manual from A to Z for households and private users, Program for TGS INTERREG-IPP Bulgaria - Macedonia 2014–2020, project "Promoting the decentralized production of energy from renewable energy sources", Ref. no. CB006.1.11.023 (EnerGAIN). http://www.ed-energy.eu/node/15

16. Integrated energy and climate plan of the republic of Bulgaria 2021–2030, ministry of energy, ministry of environment and water

17. Plamen, A., Angelov, M Blagoev Momchedjikov, "Measurement and correction of the total harmonic distortion", SIELA 2009, 4–6 June 2009, Burgas, 1, pp. 30–36 (2009) ISBN 978–954–323–530–8

18. Plamen, A., Angelov, "Modified electronic system for control the low frequency bridge inverter – part.1 block diagram". Ann. J. Electron. Sofia (2011). ISSN 1313–1842, 5, pp. 212–213

19. Angelov,P A.: Measurement and control of total harmonic distortion in frequency range 0, 02–10 khz", Electronics' 2005, 21 – 23 September, Sozopol, BULGARIA, ISBN 954 438 519 3, том.3, стр. 150 – 154

20. Мацанков М., Краткосрочно прогнозиране на електрическите товари, Издателство на ТУ – София 2019г. ISBN 978–619–167–357–5

21. Пламен А. Ангелов, „Симулация на малка PV система монтирана в градска среда - част.1", Международна научна конференция "Дигитални трансформации, медии и обществено включване, БСУ Бургас, 2020, ISBN 978–619–7126–92–1, стр.432–436

22. Мацанков М., М. Иванова, Енергиен одит за изграждане на хибридна система, Известия на ТУ – Сливен, № 1, 2019 г. ISSN 1312–3920, стр. 40 – 43

23. Matsankov, M.: Study of the short-circuit currents in branches of distribution networks with trilateral power suplliy, TechSys 2019" – Engineering, Technologies and Systems – Technical University of Sofia, Plovdiv branch 16–18 may 2019, SCOPUS. https://iopscience.iop.org/issue/1757-899X/618/1

24. Matsankov, M., Ivanova, M.: Selection of optimal variant of hybrid system under conditions of uncertainty. In: The 2nd International Conference on Electrical Engineering and Green EnergyRoma, Italy, June 28–30 2019, SCOPUS. https://www.e3s-conferences.org/articles/e3sconf/abs/2019/41/contents/contents.html. https://www.e3sconferences.org/articles/e3sconf/abs/2019/41/e3sconf_ceege18_01007/e3sconf_ceege18_01007.html. https://www.researchgate.net/publication/335545989_Selection_of_Optimal_Variant_of_Hybrid_System_under_Conditions_of_Uncertainty?fbclid=IwAR2X_Kki1b23Sb2sq6KBXJam2rcFt1gLskXLgiMnlFnjRBoqPfOl-EzfNjM

# Algorithm for the Control of Intelligent Hybrid Systems for the Production of Electric and Thermal Energy

Kamen Seymenliyski[✉], Atanas Yovkov, Radoslav Simionov, Silvia Letskovska,
Radostin Dolchinkov, Nikolina Dragneva, Eldar Zaerov, and Ginko Georgiev

Faculty of Computer Science and Engineering, Burgas Free University, Burgas, Bulgaria
{kdimitrov,silvia,rado,dragneva,ggeorgiev}@bfu.bg

**Abstract.** The aim of the study is to minimize the losses and costs of electricity and heat consumption through an intelligent integrated grid (IIM) management algorithm to control the switching process between energy sources in real time, taking into account the needs of consumption and production of electricity and heat. Solving this case study will help the future construction of smart grids. This paper presents an efficient approach for intelligent integrated grid (IIG) modeling and optimization. The main goal is the development of an algorithm for an intelligent system for remote energy management of the building, which is responsible for the effective control of the operation of the IIM. Specifically, we consider a system consisting of a rooftop solar PV installation, heat pumps for heating and cooling, energy storage units, domestic hot water heaters, meters and loads. IIMs are used to meet the electrical needs of occupants, taking into account the operational flexibility of thermal loads, which include heating, cooling and domestic hot water needs. Emphasis is placed on the optimal operation of the IIM, aiming to ensure an energy balance between production and loads (electrical and thermal). An algorithm has been introduced to manage the power supply of all components, as well as control the energy from the supplier's electrical network.

**Keywords:** Renewable energy sources · Hybrid · Intelligent energy system · Optimization · Integrated grid · Smart cities

## 1 Introduction

The development of our civilization has led to rapid pollution of the environment and depletion of energy resources. The world community is faced with the need to take serious measures to reduce energy consumption both in industry and in the residential sphere. Saving energy resources is crucial for all sectors of our lives.

Two areas for increasing the energy efficiency of facilities are of particular importance:

– saving energy resources by minimizing energy consumption and energy losses, incl. Disposal of energetically valuable waste in the public and production sector;

© The Author(s), under exclusive license to Springer Nature Switzerland AG 2022
B. Shishkov and A. Lazarov (Eds.): ICTRS 2022, CCIS 1730, pp. 85–97, 2022.
https://doi.org/10.1007/978-3-031-23226-8_7

– use of renewable energy sources in the operation of residential buildings.

The total area of building stock in the Republic of Bulgaria is about 261 million m2 of which 75% is related to the residential building stock, and the rest refers to the service sector. In total, there are about 3 million dwellings, of which about 45% are multi-family buildings and 55% in single-family houses.

Electricity has the largest share in energy consumption in residential buildings (48.3%). The other sources are biomass (23%), district heating (15%), coal, natural gas and oil, which have a smaller share.

Heating accounts for the largest share of energy consumption in households. Corresponds to an average of almost 60% of the total energy consumption. The consumption of domestic hot water is equal to almost 6% of the sweat consumption of residential buildings. Cooling consumes about 5% of the housing stock. All this leads to a share of nearly 40% of carbon emissions related to electricity used for domestic needs.

The study presents approaches to significantly reduce energy consumption in residential buildings. It is based on actual activities of building a photovoltaic plant and creating and implementing an algorithm for intelligent management of energy flows in the residential building.

## 2   Intelligent Hybrid System

Effective management of energy systems is an important task in the energy policy of many countries in connection with global warming and the significant increase in the prices of traditional energy sources [1]. Managing energy flows in such systems is a complex task, as it depends on various factors [2]. In addition, the power system management process, as well as the power source selection, must be performed in real-time mode to ensure maximum balance between supplier and consumer. The work proposes an intelligent hybrid energy system with renewable energy sources, the functioning of which is based on the forecast of the consumption and production of electricity in the system [3–5]. Based on the model, energy systems can form a forecast for consumption, production of electricity, as well as generate an optimal strategy for switching between the sources of electricity in the system.

Under an intelligent hybrid energy system with renewable energy sources, we will understand an energy system that combines traditional and renewable energy sources in one system, using devices that apply intelligent algorithms to control the necessary processes. Intelligent management is an important concept that is a deep integration of new generation information technology, new generation artificial intelligence technology and advanced power generation technology. It covers the creation of equipment for the production of energy from renewable sources, the planning, design, construction of intelligent integrated networks.

## 2.1 The Structure of an Intelligent Hybridpower Systems

The studied hybrid energy system includes the following components: photovoltaic panels (1); hybrid inverter (2); intelligent controller for managing energy flows (3); operating panel (4); buffer vessel (5); buffer vessel control controller (6); heat pump (7); heating (8); energy consumers(9); weather station (10) is shown in Fig. 1.

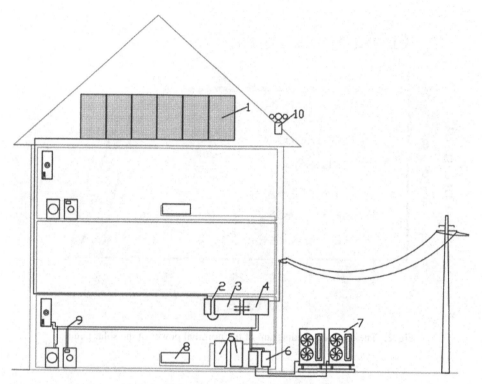

**Fig. 1.** Structure of a smart hybrid energy system

## 2.2 Characteristics of the Main Components the System

External electrical network.
The external power grid is connected to the system in case of insufficient power of other sources (eg. solar panels).

Smart controller.
Intelligent controller for managing energy flows. Collects analyzes and compares all necessary data. Manages all energy flows according to preset priorities [6].

Photovoltaic module (PV).

A photovoltaic panel is characterized by a nominal power [7]. The nominal power characterizes the amount of electricity that the photovoltaic module can produce under optimal conditions. The rated output of a solar panel depends on the solar irradiance and the temperature of the top of the panel. The diagram of the dependence of the nominal power of the solar panel 100 W on the solar radiation, provided that the temperature of the surface of the panel is 25 C, is shown in Fig. 2.

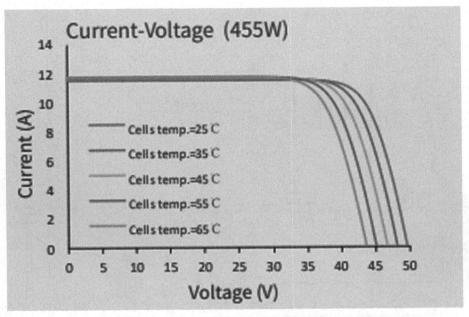

**Fig. 2.** The dependence diagram of the nominal power of the solar panel

Hybrid inverter.
In order to convert the direct current generated by the photovoltaic modules into sinusoidal alternating current, an inverter is required [8]. The main technical characteristics of the inverter are the input and output voltage, output frequency and power. A high-quality inverter must provide high efficiency and stabilization of the output voltage, low harmonic coefficient and the ability to withstand possible overloads, Fig. 3.

Weather station.
The meteorological station (can be digital) is a complex for daily monitoring of weather, temperature, pressure and humidity. Meteorological data for the entire time of its use are stored in the memory of the weather station. Meteorological data is used to forecast electricity production from solar panels.

Operation panel.
A switch is a mechanism controlled by a controller that switches energy flows in accordance with commands received from the server.

| Model | SUNSYNK-8K-SG01LP1 / SUNSYNK-8K-SG03LP1 |
|---|---|
| Product Type | Hybrid Inverter |
| Enclosure | IP65 |
| Ambient Temperature | -45°C ~ 60°C (>45°C derating) |
| Protection Level | Class I |
| **Charge Mode** | |
| Battery Voltage | 48Vd.c (40Vd.c ~ 60Vd.c) |
| Battery Current | 190Ad.c (max.) |
| AC Input Voltage | L/N/PE 220/230Va.c |
| AC Input Frequency | 50/60Hz |
| AC Input Rated Current | 36.4Aa.c |
| Max. AC Input Current | 40Aa.c (max.) |
| Max. AC Input Power | 8800W |
| Max. Apparent Output Power | 8800VA |
| PV Input Voltage | 370Vd.c (125Vd.c ~ 500Vd.c) |
| MPPT Input Voltage | 150Vd.c ~ 425Vd.c |
| PV Input Current | 22Ad.c + 22Ad.c |
| Max. PV Input Power | 10400W |
| Max. PV Isc | 28Ad.c + 28Ad.c |
| **Utility-Interactive** | |
| AC Output Voltage | L/N/PE 220/230Va.c |
| AC Output Frequency | 50/60Hz |
| AC Output Rated Current | 36.4Aa.c |
| Max. AC Output Current | 40Aa.c (max.) |
| Max. AC Output Power | 8800W |
| AC Output Rated Power | 8800VA |
| AC Output Power Factor | 0.95 leading to 0.95 lagging |
| Max. AC Isc | 145Aa.c |
| Battery Discharge Voltage | 40Vd.c ~ 60Vd.c |
| Battery Discharge Current | 190Ad.c (max.) |
| Battery Discharge Power | 8000W |
| **Stand Alone** | |
| AC Output Voltage | L/N/PE 220/230Va.c |
| AC Output Frequency | 50/60Hz |
| AC Output Rated Current | 36.4Aa.c |
| AC Output Rated Power | 8800W |
| Max. Continuous AC Passthrough Current | 50Aa.c |
| Peak Output Power | 16000W (10 seconds) |
| Battery Discharge Voltage | 40Vd.c ~ 60Vd.c |
| Max. Discharge Current | 190A (max.) |
| Compliance | VDE-AR-N 4105:1028-11; DINVDE V 0124-100:2020-06; IEC/ EN62109-1/2:2010; IEC/EN62109-1/2:2011 |

**Fig. 3.** Technical characteristics of the inverter

Controller for managing buffer vessels.

Buffer vessel management controller a controller that switches energy flows in accordance with commands coming from the intelligent energy flow management controller.

Heating system.
A system that is responsible for heating the object under study. It is controlled by the intelligent controller for managing energy flows.

Buffer vessel.
With the development of technology and the pursuit of better energy efficiency, completely new and practical home appliances have been created in home consumption [9–11]. One of them is precisely the Buffer Court. In general, it is used to temporarily store excess heat that may be generated by inert heating systems. When there is excess heat, the vessel is heated and transferred to the heating installation if necessary. Buffers can also be used when heat pumps have power outages, as well as to improve efficiency. In order to perform its function in the best way, thermal insulation is also of great importance. A good one is one that has a certificate, such as an ErP label, or when its surface is approximately the temperature of the room where the unit is installed, while the inside of the tank is about 90 degrees, Fig. 4.

**Fig. 4.** Buffer tank with ECO skin 2.0 insulation

Due to the "adherent" nature of the new ECO SKIN 2.0 insulation, heat losses are reduced by up to 47% for a buffer of 1000 L.

### 2.3  Building a Model of an Intelligent Hybrid Energy System

The photovoltaic plant is built on the roof of the residential building.
It has a power of 9.5 kWp., Fig. 5.

**Fig. 5.** Photovoltaic plant - location of the modules

Photovoltaic modules are oriented to the east, south and west. Through this arrangement of the elements, the supply of electricity to the residential building is ensured throughout the day, and not only in the hours around noon, when the sun is oriented from the south. Figure 6 and Fig. 7.

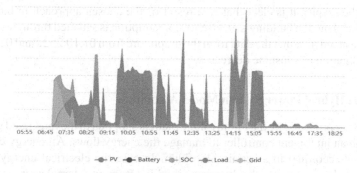

**Fig. 6.** Graph of produced and consumed electricity.

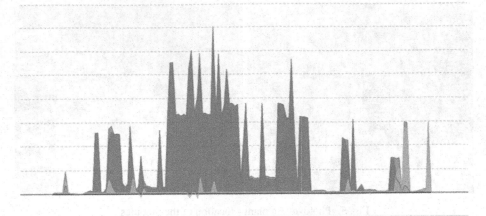

05:50  06:40  07:30  08:20  09:10  10:00  10:55  11:55  12:45  13:35  14:25  15:15  16:05  16:55  17:45  18:35  19:

—●— PV  —●— Battery  —●— SOC  —●— Load  —●— Grid

**Fig. 7.** Graph of produced and consumed electricity.

From the graphs, it is clear that as a result of the chosen approach in building the photovoltaic plant, the building's electricity consumption is satisfied throughout the day. It should be noted here that the data from the graphs are from 01.10.2022 and 02.10.2022, when the duration of sunshine decreases.

## 2.4  Smart Hybrid Power System Model Algorithm

The electricity produced by the Photovoltaic plant is supplied to the integrated grid, passing through an intelligent controller to manage the energy flows. All energy consumers are powered according to a certain algorithm. In case the electrical energy from the Solar system does not reach, the difference is added from an external source (electricity supplier) Fig. 8.

Key:

Communication lines;;
Power lines;
Components.

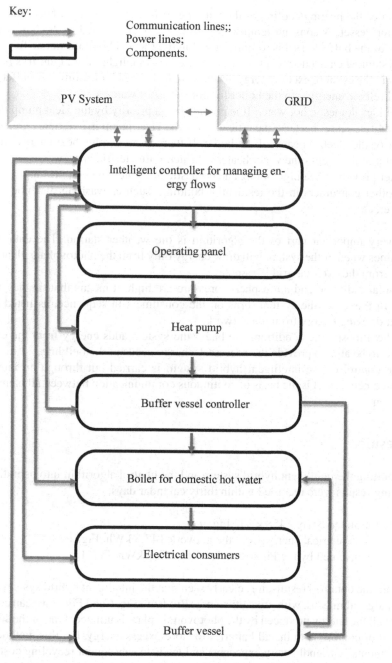

**Fig. 8.** Algorithm of intelligent hybrid system

The main goal of the system is to use the electrical energy produced by the sun as efficiently as possible. The algorithm has the following logic:

1. Ensures the heating/cooling of the building. It is carried out by a heat pump and a buffer vessel. A constant temperature of 22 C° is maintained in the building. The role of the buffer vessel is to store energy in the form of hot/cold water. To give it to a system when needed in a time when there is no sunlight or at night. It is intended that in the event of excess energy, when there is no need for heating, the buffer vessel will release energy into the boiler for domestic hot water.
2. Provides domestic hot water. It is provided as a priority by the Heat pump through the buffer vessel because the efficiency of the Heat pump is five times greater than that of the electric heater of the boiler. If there is no surplus heat energy from the heat pump system - the water heater is heated with electric energy.
3. After providing heating/cooling and domestic hot water, the system supplies energy to other consumers in the residential building, such as washing machine, clothes dryer, etc.

A very important part of the algorithm is the weather station. The data from it determines whether the system will draw energy only from the photovoltaic plant or add energy from the external grid. Example:

If solar radiation and atmospheric pressure are high, it means that the day will be sunny. In this case, the system turns on the consumers in sequence, as listed above, without drawing energy from the network.

If the atmospheric conditions are bad – the system adds energy from the external network to be able to provide the necessary energy needs of the building.

The control of the intelligent hybrid system is carried out through an intelligent integrated network. It is the basis of continuous communication between all elements in the system.

## 3   Results

After putting the intelligent hybrid system and the control algorithm into operation, the following results were recorded within thirty calendar days:

1. Total consumed energy 458 kWh, Fig. 9
2. Consumed electrical energy from the network 147.3 kWh, Fig. 10
3. Energy consumed by the Photovoltaic plant 313.3 kWh, Fig. 11

From the obtained results, it is clearly seen that the intelligent hybrid system and the control algorithm work with great efficiency. But from Fig. 6 and Fig. 7 we can conclude that not all the energy produced by the photovoltaic plant is utilized. One of the solutions to this shortcoming is to install batteries to store excess energy, but this method is not environmentally friendly, very expensive and leads to subsequent recycling costs.

For this purpose, the subject of future research and implementation will be a project to build a hydrogen production and storage system. As well as producing electricity from stored hydrogen.

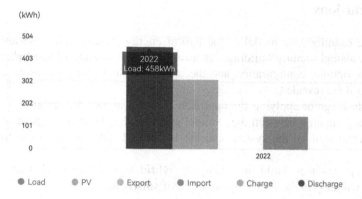

**Fig. 9.** Total consumed energy

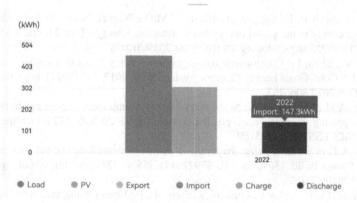

**Fig. 10.** Consumed electrical energy from the network

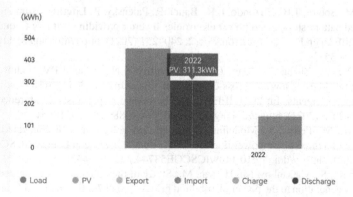

**Fig. 11.** Energy consumed by the Photovoltaic plant.

## 4   Conclusions

The article examines the model of the hybrid energy system with renewable energy sources in a single-family building. As a result of a real study of the hybrid energy system, the optimal configuration and the optimal strategy for purchasing electricity from the grid are revealed.

The advantage of applying the approach is that it allows determining the optimal strategy for switching between the external grid and the photovoltaic plant depending on the current state of the system and the forecasted state based on meteorological conditions.

The steps taken to build an intelligent hybrid system and implement a control algorithm will help in the future construction of smart cities.

## References

1. Gielen, D., Boshell, F., Saygin, D., Bazilian, M.D., Wagner, N., Gorini, R.: The role of renewable energy in the global energy transformation. Energy s Rev. **24**, pp. 38–50 (2019). ISSN 2211-467X, https://doi.org/10.1016/j.esr.2019.01.006
2. Dhaoui, M., Sbita, L.: Control and management of energy flows in a multi-source hybrid system. Int. Conf. Green Energy Convers. Syst. (GECS) **2017**, 1–6 (2017). https://doi.org/10.1109/GECS.2017.8066252
3. Eltamaly, A.M., Alotaibi, M.A.: Novel fuzzy-swarm optimization for sizing of hybrid energy systems applying smart grid concepts. IEEE Access **9**, 93629–93650 (2021). https://doi.org/10.1109/ACCESS.2021.3093169
4. Marszal, A.J., et al.: Zero energy building – a review of definitions and calculation methodologies. Energy Build. **43**(4), pp. 971–979 (2011). ISSN 0378-7788, https://doi.org/10.1016/j.enbuild.2010.12.022
5. Kanchev, H., Lu, D., Colas, F., Lazarov, V., Francois, B.: Energy management and operational planning of a microgrid with a pv-based active generator for smart grid applications. IEEE Trans. Industr. Electron. **58**(10), 4583–4592 (2011). https://doi.org/10.1109/TIE.2011.2119451
6. Stecca, M., Soeiro, T.B., Elizondo, L.R., Bauer, P., Palensky, P.: Lifetime estimation of grid-connected battery storage and power electronics inverter providing primary frequency regulation. IEEE Open J. Indus. Electron. Soc. **2**, 240–251 (2021). https://doi.org/10.1109/OJIES.2021.3064635
7. Liu, T., Xu, X., Zhang, Z., Xiao, J., Yu, Y., Jaubert, J.N.: Bifacial PV module operating temperature: high or low? A cross-comparison of thermal modeling results with outdoor on-site measurements. In: 2021 IEEE 48th Photovoltaic Specialists Conference (PVSC), pp. 2070–2073 (2021). https://doi.org/10.1109/PVSC43889.2021.9518651
8. Matsankov, M., Petrov, S.: Modeling of the induced voltage in a disconnected grounded conductor of a three-phase power line. Int. Conf. Smart City Green Energy (ICSCGE) **2021**, 75–78 (2021). https://doi.org/10.1109/ICSCGE53744.2021.9654332
9. Nedeltcheva, S., Matsankov, M., Hassan, M.: Study of the options for joining decentralized electricity generation to the power distribution grid. In: 2020 7th International Conference on Energy Efficiency and Agricultural Engineering (EE&AE), pp. 1–4 (2020). https://doi.org/10.1109/EEAE49144.2020.9279073

10. Beloev, H., Stoyanov, I., Iliev, T.: Good practices in implementing energy efficiency measures in "Angel Kanchev" university of ruse. In: 2022 8th International Conference on Energy Efficiency and Agricultural Engineering (EE&AE), pp. 1–4 (2022). https://doi.org/10.1109/EEAE53789.2022.9831424

11. Aprilya, A., Mayarakaca, M.C., Briantoro, H., Moegiharto, Y.: Energy efficiency in D2D cooperative communication system UAV-assisted for energy harvesting process at source and relay. In: 2022 International Electronics Symposium (IES), pp. 199–203 (2022). https://doi.org/10.1109/IES55876.2022.9888427

# Author Index

Printed in the United States
by Baker & Taylor Publisher Services

Printed in the United States
by Baker & Taylor Publisher Services